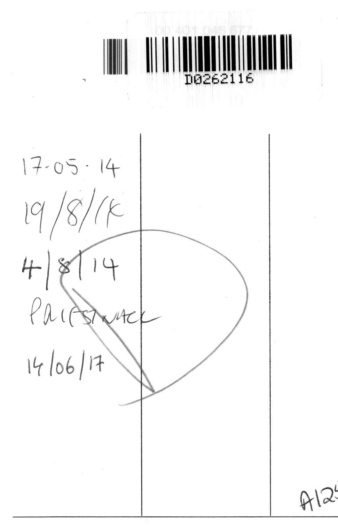

D0262116

17·05·14

19/8/1K

4/8/14

PAIFSTNACK

14/06/17

A125

Please return / renew this item by last
date shown. Books may also be renewed
by phone or the Internet.

Northamptonshire Libraries and Information Service

Northamptonshire
County Council

www.northamptonshire.gov.uk/catalogue

IT SHOULDN'T HAPPEN TO A MIDWIFE

As the Swinging Sixties continue, Jane Yeadon is ready to start her training as a midwife. With general nursing already under her belt, it's time for a whole new adventure. When she arrives at the Royal Maternity Hospital in Belfast, Jane soon meets a host of new and intriguing characters. As well as the usual glacial matron who can turn tears to ice, Jane makes friends with fellow nurses Timid Marie, English Cynthia and Strong-minded Margaret, and together they tackle the challenges ahead and discover that there are very few straightforward births in the maternity business and an awful lot to learn.

IT SHOULDN'T HAPPEN
TO A MIDWIFE

It Shouldn't Happen To A Midwife

by

Jane Yeadon

Magna Large Print Books
Long Preston, North Yorkshire,
BD23 4ND, England.

British Library Cataloguing in Publication Data.

Yeadon, Jane
 It shouldn't happen to a midwife.

 A catalogue record of this book is
 available from the British Library

 ISBN   978-0-7505-3708-7

First published in Great Britain in 2012 by
Black & White Publishing Ltd.

Copyright © Jane Yeadon 2012

Cover illustration © mirrorpix

Published in Large Print 2013 by arrangement with
Black & White Publishing

Magna Large Print is an imprint of Library Magna Books Ltd.

Printed and bound in Great Britain by
T.J. (International) Ltd., Cornwall, PL28 8RW

To Gemma, Eileen and Deirdre,
my Irish sisters.

CONTENTS

ACKNOWLEDGEMENTS

Thanks to the Black & White Publishing team for their faith, and the Belfast babies for their mothers.

1

A NEW ARRIVAL

The hand came from nowhere. It slapped over my mouth. A second later, I was yanked from prime site to the back of the huge crowds lining Belfast's Falls Road.

'Are ye mad? Mother of God, what d'you think you're doing?' My friend Seonaid sounded frightened. Normally she'd be using the kerbside to practise tap dancing or crowd control. It must be serious. She'd just jettisoned her advisory role on all things cheerful, personal and matters of state to gag, grab and drag a spectator from the frontline.

The street was a-wheeze with the sound of pipes, flutes and accordions. Underneath, like a heartbeat, a drum thumped, so big, its carrier risked a hernia. Meanwhile the wind section, faces purple with blowing endeavour, looked in danger of self-combustion. Still, it was stirring stuff and we were off-duty student midwives (not First Aiders) enjoying an atmosphere charged with good humour and excitement.

A group of men had just strutted round the corner to join the procession. They wore bowler hats, white gloves and had badges with ribboned paraphernalia round their necks. They were rather like those decorative halters worn by Clydesdale horses at agricultural shows. Putting such eccentric-looking gear together must have given the group a lot of work.

I'd laughed in appreciation of their effort and promptly been relocated.

'Och, Seonaid!' I protested when she eventually removed her gagging hand. 'They look droll. You're not telling me they're serious?'

'Believe you me, it's no joke. They're key players in an Orange Parade. It's to show allegiance to the Crown,' she pointed her thumb as if hitching a lift, 'and a really old tradition – a celebration of King Billy winning the Battle of the Boyne. Come on! I don't trust you to keep your mouth shut. The way you're speaking you could start a riot.' Already she was dragging me away.

'So what battle was that then?'

'William of Orange beat James II. In 1690. Proddies versus Catholics really.' She'd broken into a jog.

By comparison, Scotland's 1746 blood-bath, the Battle of Culloden, was a recent event but certainly not an occasion for celebration.

I hurried after her. 'You wouldn't find a march like this in Aberdeen,' I said, thinking

14

with affection of a tolerant city, and momentarily forgetting Belfast didn't hold my old
training ground in the same regard. I should
have remembered the night I arrived.

I'd thought my taxi driver would give a big
Belfast welcome to a nurse from Aberdeen.
OK, maybe November wasn't the best time
to promote it as the Silver City with the
Golden Sands, but his take on it seemed a
little excessive.

'More like Abortion City, so it is.' Settling
jug-like ears on the mantle piece of his coat
collar, he'd spat on two fingers. He wound
down the window, doused his cigarette, then
flung it out onto the Falls Road: the one the
Orange March was now taking.

He drew up at a large, well-lit building.
'Bostock House,' he announced, 'and a quair
name for a nurses' home, so it is.' His tone
was combative as if I might argue but I was
relieved. The hearse-like cab and his manner
were so suited to the nearby cemetery I'd
thought I might be dumped there instead.

He pretended indifference but I caught
him looking pleased as, purse in hand, I
struggled out with luggage reluctant to follow. I hiked a smile over gritted teeth then
shut the door with such a slam, it echoed
down the empty road like a pistol shot.

I hadn't expected to feel defensive but
bending to speak through a window now

half closed, I gestured at the sad neon-lit street.

'So no back-street abortions here then?'

It was 1966. Aberdeen's concession to swinging still only extended to the Pill given as a contraceptive prize for marriage; but at least my old training ground was trying to put a stop to illegal, miserable and dangerous terminations with safer hospital provision.

He shrugged and pointed to a nearby sign marked Royal Maternity Hospital. 'Sure not this close anyway.'

I posted a fist of ten bobs through the window, 'Keep the change. I wouldn't want you calling it "Abermean" as well.'

His answer was a revved engine. Then he roared away. As the cab rounded the corner, the rain blurred an angry red of brake lights. Surprising, considering so little evidence of them on the way from Aldergrove Airport.

Being here at all was something of a miracle and certainly no thanks to a boyfriend who'd met me off my Aberdeen bus connection to Glasgow. Judging by the anxious way he'd consulted his watch, he was keen to ensure my onward journey even if native thrift made it tricky.

'There is an airport bus,' he'd said in such a bright way it ought to have invited suspicion, 'but it's expensive. If we just wait at this stop, we'll get the Paisley one. It'll save a few bob and take us near enough.'

I should have asked him to define near enough as the bus (late) apparently bent on making up time, gathered speed approaching the airport, then whizzed past with complete disregard for all appeals to stop. Had it not been for the combination of a slowing roundabout and the ability to get off in the running position whilst catching suitcases thoughtfully thrown out by the boyfriend now demoted to mere acquaintance, I might have missed that plane and all its waiting passengers.

Responding to their universal sigh as the last one tumbled aboard, the air hostess quietly closed the door behind me with a mild, 'Well she's here now. Now, would yez all belt up?'

There was hardly time to enjoy being airborne. Only enough to glimpse land below, so green, it was easy to see why it was called the Emerald Isle. Then we'd landed and I'd got that taxi.

Now, thanks to that driver and thoroughly grounded, I checked around, seeing a church poking one finger heavenward whilst surrounding low buildings crouched serf-like, humble in close, wire-meshed confabs. They looked as dismal as judgemental neighbours. By comparison, the home was big, bright and welcoming in clean-lined modernity.

Since Aberdeen had so prompted the taxi

driver's disapproval, I thought I'd say I'd trained in Inverness. Who was to know?

Lie at the ready, I opened the door.

'Well, well! Last but not least eh? Sure if it's not the wee nurse from Aberdeen.'

A figure on skinny legs and stilettos burst from a small kiosk-like office at the entrance of a hall, which, with its high ceiling and shiny floor, had the barren feel of an ice rink. Now she was skating across it and going fast. Her bust and head, crowned by something resembling a rookery, made her look top heavy, as if she'd to run to keep up with her front.

I thought we'd have a collision, but she pulled up just in time.

'Sure and it must be Nurse Macpherson!' Bosoming frills quivered whilst her bangled hand pumped mine, 'and may I just, right here and now, welcome you to the shores of Ulster, UK.' The bracelet charms clinked as her other hand rooted about in her hair, red varnished nails darting like fish amongst weeds.

'I'm Miss MacCready, spelt with one "a" and two "C's" and I'm *the* Home Receptionist, and completely responsible for the comfort and safety of all you girls living here, and of course,' she gestured at the office, 'in charge of your security, keys and mail.' Her huge spectacles magnified eyes fanned with laughter lines and gleaming with a manic energy I couldn't comprehend; but then I'd been travelling all day with morning and home surely a lifetime away.

Indifferent to my travel fatigue, Miss Mac-Cready powered on. 'Would you ever wait till I get me pen? Ah ha! Here we are!' In triumph she located one from her nest of hair and spoke to it as if it were a naughty child. 'I wondered where you'd gone, you useless article. To be sure you'll be pleased that's everybody accounted for now – thanks be to God and you'll get to bed soon too. Let's go!'

She tucked her blouse into the back of a heroically short skirt then glided down a corridor leading off the hall. There was a listed sheet of paper headed 'Fresh Student Midwives' taped to the wall beside a lift garlanded with bright buttons. Two girls stood beside it,

'All correct now.' With a flourish, Miss MacCready ticked off my name, consulted the biro then sent it back to the rookery. 'You're a great wee operator, so you are!'

The lift looked a lot safer and was modern compared to the mantrap hiding in a dark corner of the Aberdeen nurses' home, yet one of the girls was gazing at it with terror. The other had the bored air of a seasoned traveller. Amongst the jumble of luggage surrounding them, the smart liveried stuff with its double-barrelled name tag was probably hers.

Miss MacCready threw out her arms, impresario-like. 'And would you not say that's great timing? These girls here are fresh too so you'll all be going the same way.' She pointed heavenward then produced a key, presenting it as if conferring an honour. 'Now, Nurse Macpherson. This is all yours, and for the whole of next year! Room seven-hundred fourteen – top floor. You'll get a grand view to be sure.'

A small hand fluttered over nervous Miss Mouse's mouth but not in time to muffle a squeak. 'Top floor? Is that where we're going? Mother of God! I was so scared seeing this big place, sure I wasn't paying attention and here I am and not even a head for heights.' She glanced at the key jingling in her hand. 'And I've got seven-hundred thirteen! Sacred Heart of God. Thirteen now!'

'There's one good thing and that's I now know who my neighbour is. I'll be next door. Hello, I'm Jane.'

Unsure of Irish formality, I twiddled my fingers then stuck out my hand into which hers, quivering and cold as a landed tiddler, fell. A wan smile flickered. 'This place is so big. How d'you look so confident. Are you not just terrified of getting lost?'

'Not really, but I certainly don't feel *fresh*,' I said, nodding at the heading on the new students' list, but the quip was lost.

'I'm alright that way,' she said in a voice soft as rain. 'It didn't take too long to get here. Actually, Cynthia and I arrived at the same time.'

'But not off the same boat, Marie.' Cynthia's laugh was cool. She was tall with a splendid nose, down which, on account of our stunted growth and proximity, she had to squint. 'Though we seem to be in one now, so come along, do. Sorry I'm holding the controls, you'll have to take the handshake as read.' She had a conductor finger pressed over the lift button whilst holding up a key in her other hand. 'And it appears I'm a neighbour too but look, sorry to sound impatient, but we really must be getting on. You might not have been travelling all day, but I have.'

The lift arrived with smooth efficiency. Cynthia stepped inside keeping the door open with a large best-leather and shining-shod foot. Pocketing her key, she leant forward to pick up her luggage as if it were lightweight.

'Are you coming or not?' She sounded exasperated as Marie and I struggled with our own loads. 'I would like to get settled in before midnight.'

She gave a world-weary sigh but the receptionist was unfazed, responding only by clapping her hands, checking her watch and trilling. 'Well then if you hurry you should

21

just make it, and even though you're the last girls to arrive, the best room hasn't been taken yet and I'm thinking, Nurse Fitzwilliam, you might just be the lucky one. Number or not.' She touched Marie lightly on the arm and gave a scream of laughter. 'When you see it, you'll be saying it's the luck of the Irish.'

Marie looked disbelieving and Cynthia thoughtful. The latter said, 'Is there a penalty to being English then?'

Miss MacCready kicked in the last few pieces of luggage and gave a carefree twirl. 'Not at all. It's not as if you can help it.' She chuckled then tucked away a few nesting-down twigs, adjusted her spectacles, lowered her head and glided away, the sounds of, 'Goodnight, goodnight. God bless,' floating in her wake.

Cynthia took her foot in to let the lift doors close. 'Peasant!' she sighed. She leant back, glared at us, raised her eyebrows and tapped her head on the wall as if it soothed her. 'Coming from The London Hospital was a long trip. The least I was expecting was to meet somebody normal.'

2

MEET AND GREET

'Holy Mother!' Marie backed into the corner, clasped her hands and closed her eyes.

As if rocket powered, the lift shot straight to the top. Then, with the same formidable efficiency, the doors opened in a whisper.

I stumbled out. 'What're the signs and symptoms of the bends?' I wondered. 'And I suppose if we asked, maybe we could get our stomachs back come morning.'

Marie had followed. 'Ah, Jane, it's you that's the joker, so you are, but that's not a lift, it's space travel. I never thought it'd be so quick or easy.' She swung around in wonder as she took in the bright corridor, with its rooms on either side, broken up by occasional sitting areas with easy-chairs in gossip groups. 'Ah now, girls! It's a miracle! So modern and all, and look! There's even a kitchen.'

Some girls were coming out of a pantry area, mugs in hand, which they waved before heading for a lounge area. 'Come and have a cup of tay when you've settled in. We're new too,' they called. They looked friendly and already quite at home.

'I rather think I'll be going straight to bed,' Cynthia's cool voice fluted back, 'but if number thirteen makes you nervous, Marie, I'll easily swap.' She strode down the corridor with the confidence of a matron on a ward round.

There was something about her that invited challenge and her remark about the lack of normal people niggled. Whilst Marie didn't seem to notice, somebody else had.

'Whoa, there!' I held a hand up in a gesture a traffic policeman might have admired. 'Why don't you have a look at it first, Marie? It might have good views. Miss MacCready wanted you to have it. You wouldn't want to disappoint her.'

Cynthia plunked down her cases and planted her feet. She adjusted her Alice band as if to free horns then tucked her blonde hair behind her ears. Her nostrils flared. 'It's only a suggestion. *Un*lucky numbers can really spook some people and realising Marie's worries I was only trying to help.'

But Marie wasn't listening. All her attention was fixed on the door. 'Girls!' It came as a plea. 'Maybe it's an omen. I don't know if I can put one foot past the other now and did I not mention my fear? Vertigo it is alright.' She chewed a finger and blinked hard.

'You don't say.' But my irony was lost. She

kept on looking so petrified even I had a momentary qualm before taking her key, turning the lock and throwing the door open.

She inched cautiously into the room, its light wood and modern fittings making it as bright and comfortable as any hotel room.

'Jasus!'

'I just hope mine's like this.' Cynthia made it sound like a flaw. 'If it's not, I'll be asking if there's a difference in the rent.'

But in a rush of confidence Marie had gone over to the bed, patting the pale blue bed cover eiderdown as if to check it was really there. 'Even if there is, it'd be worth it. I can't believe my eyes, all this space for just me!' She clapped her hands then pointed. 'And, look! Would you not say there's another miracle! A place for Our Lady.' She rummaged around in her suitcase and took out a small statue which she held with the care of an antique dealer handling fenced goods.

Cynthia raised her eyebrows into perfect arches. 'You mean to put that on the bookshelf? Won't that leave you short of space for your paperwork and textbooks?'

'Well, there's still plenty room for them too,' I said, wishing Cynthia would pipe down and wondering if the ornament was Ireland's version of Florence Nightingale. 'She'll look well there, but shouldn't she have a lamp in her hand instead of that plate on her head?'

'That's a halo,' Cynthia said, shooting out a withering look, but Marie's puzzled expression went as she crossed over to a wide window. She pulled back the swirly patterned curtains, uttering little cries of wonder. 'And the views! I can't believe the views.'

In the glow of city light Belfast was darkly sulking under a pall of fine drizzle and smoke. Probably the winter light didn't help but it looked big, ugly and industrial with cranes gobbing at every corner. Surrounding hills might have softened the view but right now they were scowling like unattractive heavies. Still, the scene might improve in the morning light and since it appeared to have cured Marie's vertigo, I couldn't help but be infected by her happiness.

'Yes, it's a fine sight. Nay problem. You're sorted. Looks as if you're going to be fine, Marie. And what about you, Cynthia, have you much to unpack?' Even if she had a very savvy way I felt I should ask. After all, we were supposed to be members of a caring profession.

'No. I'm used to travelling light. Actually, I've done a fair amount of getting about so I've got it down to a fine art.' She gave a modest cough. 'When work could spare me in London I'd pop over to Paris to visit the parents. They moved there a few years ago.

Daddy's in the property business and–'

Cynthia's life history was cut short as a leprechaun knocked on the door and danced in, bringing the tea drinkers with her. They looked about with a benign interest.

'Well, hello there! I'd say this is another grand place for a party – that is, of course, if you like parties, but sure, doesn't everybody?' The sprite's face was chalk white, her green eyes full of mischief.

Marie looked shocked. 'Oh!' She clasped her hands. 'Parties! When on earth will we have time for those? They say midwifery training's awful hard – desperate!'

'It's just a matter of application and hard work,' said one girl, her eye makeup at odds with the tired grey cardigan tenting her from the neck down. 'When I was standing in for Sister in theatre, it was a worry until I got a bit of experience, then it was so easy I could have done it blindfolded. I'm Margaret, by the way.' She wrung our hands in a no-nonsense way.

Resisting all her attempts to flatten it, the imp's hair stood up in black spikes. 'Ach now, eyesight's a quair and handy thing but I'm sure these girls are not wanting to be hearing any of that oulde theatre stuff you're always on about. Are we not all beginners again?' She spoke lightly and hopped on dancer's legs to the window to see out. 'Some view! We're lucky – some of the others look over the other side onto the hospital grounds. It's grand too – particularly if you're interested in hen houses pretending to be annexes.' She scrubbed her nose. 'They set off the general hospital and maternity nicely!'

She opened the window and, ignoring Marie's squeals, leant out. A chill wind piled in carrying with it the sound of traffic passing far below. 'Would you think anybody out there might be heading for a bit of fun? Maybe even the theatre.' Closing the window, she turned back. 'Not your kind, of course, Margaret,' she said, crossing her fingers in both hands and holding them aloft as if to do the Highland Fling, 'but the fun kind. I wouldn't be wanting much of the other.'

'I'm pretty sure it'll be difficult to avoid,' Cynthia spoke up, straightening and addressing the troops. 'This maternity hospital only accepts births which might prove difficult. Of course, theatre experience will be tremendously useful. I'm jolly glad I've had plenty of it.'

Margaret looked at her thoughtfully and stuck out her chin. 'And where would you have done your training then?'

'The London Hospital.'

'And which would that be?' asked the imp, idly examining her fingernails.

'I'd have thought everybody knows about *The* London Hospital. It's got such a wonderful reputation. Surely you must have heard of it.'

'I can't say I have,' said Margaret, 'but maybe that's because we girls,' she gestured at the group, 'were so busy thinking we'd a grand training where we were.' She took a deep breath, making the tent billow. 'Isn't that right?'

The others nodded vigorously whilst the imp put in, 'Mind you, I'd have to say, excepting yourself, *Sister* Margaret, the Royal let us go very easily.'

'Some easier than others,' a cheerful butterball of a girl spoke up. 'What about the blood, Seonaid?'

The imp waved a careless hand. 'Ach, Lorna, you'll be meaning the blood transfusion? Just because I didn't get straightaway to the fridge and eight bags turned into liver? And after all the fuss, didn't I get my whole family to sign up as blood donors. They were a perfect match, all eight of them.'

Whilst I hoped Seonaid's family wasn't her size or there'd be nothing left of them, Cynthia gave a disbelieving laugh. 'I presume you mean the match was numerical?'

'That too,' Seonaid said carelessly. 'Anybody can make a mistake. Anyway, you're not so perfect yourself, Lorna. Was it not yourself who set off the fire alarm when a medical student got too close?'

'Had to put out the flame somehow,'

laughed Lorna, patting her bun as if to stop it escaping. Even if her clothes were dowdy, she had the air of a mischievous cherub with rosy cheeks and blue eyes magnified by spectacles, full of fun. 'I was doing him a favour.' She cocked a bright look on Marie and myself. 'So where did youse train then?'

Marie sighed and brushed away a tear. 'G-galway.' She made it sound like Brigadoon. 'I loved it but I wasn't anything special there, not like Margaret and Cynthia with all that theatre experience.'

Both girls took her respect as a matter of course whilst the others turned to me.

'Aberdeen.' I tried to mumble it.

'Ah, sure now, we've all heard of Aberdeen,' crowed the imp and did a little skip.

3

A MATRON CALLS

'I've got two tickets for a Showband tonight. Would you fancy coming?' Unlike some, Seonaid had slept well, was fully refreshed and jumping with energy. Just watching her skips and leaps was exhausting.

'For Heaven's sake! Would you settle down now? Sure this is only our first morn' and already you're planning heading out for an evening of fun. Let's concentrate on finding the lecture room instead.' Margaret spoke with the command of a theatre sister about to get the team concentrating on the fascinations of a swab count.

We'd breakfasted in the Home's dining room. It led directly from the reception area and with its big light-filled space, pine panelling and chrome service area, was more like a large restaurant. It also catered for the general hospital so the place was full of other users, marked by their different uniforms and busy in conversation.

We, however, had to be somewhere else. Margaret might not have had a seniority badge but we trooped behind her as, assuming natural leadership, she led the way.

Miss MacCready had given directions to the maternity hospital. 'Through from the dining room and straight ahead. The classroom's as easy to find as the nose on your face.'

Dressed in green, designed to dazzle and arguing with the night porter about a key, the receptionist was an easier find than this room, a poor relation tucked by the back door of the maternity unit and reached by a covered concrete job of a walkway. There were silo-like changing rooms off it. They were for the non-resident Belfast girls, some of whom had now joined us in the classroom and were about to take seats. Like us, they wore blue uniforms with aprons tied in crosses at the back.

Margaret pulled on hers, hawser-like and checked her sausage curls were still in curfew zone under her cap. Her lipstick was smudged. Maybe wearing a theatre mask blunted makeup skills below eye level. Undaunted, she said, 'I was thinking, Seonaid, it's early enough to be gadding about and maybe we should be giving some thought to these instead.' As she passed it she nodded at a blackboard where the words 'Lie', 'Attitude' and 'Position' were written, then she moved to stake a claim on the front row.

'That's the first lecture of the day over then.' I joined Seonaid, who'd made a beeline to the back. 'Mind these words do look kind of interesting but not half as much as – what did you call it?'

'Showband. Had you not any in Sin City?'

'Pipe Bands,' I said, remembering their skirl and finding it hard to equate the memory of them playing in the Union Street Gardens with vice or fast living. 'I'm beginning to wonder if there was a side of the city that I never saw but wish I had.'

'Well I've never been there. Still, I'm thinking you've taken a bit of granite over with you. See?' Seonaid nodded at Margaret and Cynthia who, square-jawed, were vying for position nearest the lectern. Lorna was sitting behind them and giving them the attention of someone studying life under the microscope.

'The apron ties make them look like a pair of St Andrew's flags too, but from the back I suppose we all do

'But they'll be the biggest.' Seonaid patted her knees as if encouraging them to grow then leant forward. 'Sweet Jesus! Why would you want to be sitting so near the front? It's right under the line of fire!' She shook her head. 'Not for me – that's for sure.'

'Me neither,' sighed Marie, sliding in beside us. 'And where do they get that poise? They're both so full of it.' She pulled on her earlobe, her first and most definite action glimpsed since arrival. 'And are they not just made to be matrons now?'

'Built for it for sure but they're bound to improve. Anyway,' Seonaid angled her head towards Marie and momentarily pulled one knee as if limbering up, 'I'll tell you something that's more important, and that's you should stop all this worrying. Have you not qualified to be a state registered nurse? You're every bit the same as all of us here. And was that not a lot to cope with?' She sucked her lips and scissored her ankles. 'Now that was stressful. D'you know, before my finals I even gave up a whole month's dancing.'

'Sssshh!' Marie rolled her eyes as a tutor

33

strode into the room.

She was so like my favourite no-nonsense Edinburgh auntie with her brisk walk, precise Scots accent and corrugated iron hair I sat up, surprised, and rubbed my eyes.

'Good morning, Nurses. And a very warm welcome to The Royal Maternity Hospital.' She was tall and wore a cap banded the same green as her dress. Her gaze had the look of approval you'd give to a tray of finely-baked scones. 'I'm Miss Harvey and I'm your main tutor. You will have others but your training is my responsibility, which won't be too much of a challenge, I imagine, given that you're all registered nurses and as such, know the payoff of study, endeavour and professional behaviour.'

It was so like a precursor to a temperance and morals homily, I'd to check it really wasn't Auntie Rita giving a pre-holiday lecture – but Miss Harvey was real enough. In her own tutorial right she turned to the blackboard and tapped the three words there. 'I'll be discussing these with you as soon as you swear your oath of allegiance. Matron should be coming in to oversee this formality as well as to meet you. She'll be any minute now.'

She consulted her fob watch, the wall clock for good measure, then looked around. 'So as we've got a minute or two this might be a good chance to practise a bit of public speaking through introductions because, as you probably know, part of your training will be running antenatal classes. I need to make sure you're comfortable and clear doing this.'

There was a squeak of horror from Marie which was easily traced. 'Let's start with you, shall we? Just a little personal stuff, please. No more than a few words.'

Reluctantly Marie stood up, face crimson. 'I'm from Tip-pip-erary – and me name's Mary.' She gave a hysterical giggle, blew her nose and sat down.

Miss Harvey glimmered. 'Well that was certainly brief and to the point, Mary.'

Cynthia's hand shot up. 'She's actually Marie.'

Miss Harvey's gaze fell upon Cynthia; her tone was cool. 'Apart from her advisor, you would be?'

Cynthia cleared her throat, stood up and advanced. 'It's probably best for voice delivery,' she explained, elbowing the tutor aside. Then, placing her hands on the lectern, she addressed the class in full oratory mode. 'I'm Miss Brown-Smythe – spelt with a "Y" – and I'm here today because I see midwifery training as an essential part of career progression in a caring profession of which I am proud to be a member. Now I don't want to take over,' she tucked her hair behind her ear then encompassed everybody with a grand sweep of her hand, 'but I'd be happy to take any questions about myself from the floor.'

'Thank you, Nurse Smythe, I'm sure there'll be plenty opportunity for that in the future but right now, unfortunately, we haven't that much time for such an honour.' Miss Harvey turned to Margaret who was straining at the leash.

I tuned out knowing she would be as big a gas bag as Cynthia and wondered what I should say.

Everybody said midwifery was hard work but I needed the qualification to be that district nurse which had always been the ultimate goal. The idea of caring for people well away from scary matrons and strict sisters held great appeal.

Surely birth couldn't be all that complicated even if doom-mongering colleagues in other training schools swore that studying to become a midwife was on a par with, if not worse than, actual labour. I wondered how career-minded girls bent on a child-free future would know.

Anyway, Belfast was sure to present a colourful change, an exciting prospect and somewhere far away where a bit of fun and adventure might soften the necessary training. I supposed I could hardly say that though.

'Girl with the red hair, please.'

'I'm Jane Macpherson and I trained in Aberdeen.'

Gales of laughter swept the classroom. I looked round, astonished by the reaction.

Miss Harvey was cool. 'I've never thought of Aberdeen as being hysterically funny.'

'It's just that Jane sounds like Janet in the telly's *Dr Finlay's Casebook*,' Margaret said, wiping her eyes with a man-sized hanky. 'It's amazing. So like that cute old housekeeper.'

'Wonderful, I'm sure, but I imagine she's her own person. Ah!' She started. 'Matron! Sorry we didn't hear you come in.'

Some say you can grow into a job and since every district nurse I'd met was dumpy and cheerful I reckoned I was half-way there already. It was only a matter of passing midwifery to get the happy bit.

Matrons were different. Certainly the woman striding into the room, with her stiff manner, collar, cuffs and cap, looked as if she came from a heavily regulated past. Perhaps her career was influenced by crisp nannies with starch intent. Certainly, she was neither dumpy nor was she cheerful.

'I'm not surprised with all that hilarity.' She purse-strung her mouth. She spoke quietly but her uniform was so royally blue it shouted authority. 'We could hear you from my office – and that's upstairs!'

Behind Matron was someone no less important if a lot shorter. It was just as well he wore a red tie. With his measured tread and Bible clasped to his breast he could have been mistaken for an undertaker.

'Good morning, Nurses,' began Matron, adjusting her brilliantly white cuffs before clasping her hands as if in benefaction. 'For those of you not privileged enough to have been born in Ulster, let me congratulate you on coming here and choosing our fine hospital for your midwifery training.' She spoke to a distant object somewhere at the back of the lecture hall.

For a woman of indeterminate age with a job of huge responsibility, her brow was remarkably smooth and just fractionally creased as she paused to allow her companion, beadle-like, to advance on the lectern Miss Harvey was hurriedly lowering.

She took the floor again. Getting underway she spoke in the clipped tones of someone used to being listened to with respect. As I'm sure you appreciate we may only be six counties, but the North of Ireland is a different country from the South and as such we governing bodies expect you to take an oath of allegiance to this part of the United Kingdom. We need to do this right away and are pleased to have Mr Coates from Stormont, our Parliament, with us today. He has the power and, indeed, authority to oversee this ceremony.'

Ensuring everybody's attention with a

mine-sweeping gaze, she stepped back so that we could all concentrate on a lectern now occupied by a Bible capped with the bushy eyebrows of a very small person. 'So, without further ado, I'll hand over to him.'

'Oh, wait a wee minute.' Miss Harvey stooped to further adjust the stand.

'Thank you,' he said curtly as if resenting her height, then, spearing his elbows enough to allow him leverage, he leant forward and tapped the Bible. 'Now, I'm presuming nobody here has a problem taking this oath because if you do, this's the time to say so.' The eyebrows waggled like busy caterpillars.

A short silence was broken by Cynthia who put up her hand as if halting a convoy.

'Yes?'

She held an eloquent silence, then drawled, 'Even if I do come from across the water, I'm a British citizen and, as such, a loyal subject, so I'm not clear why I need to take this pledge, and I'm sure I'm speaking for everyone else.' Like a general mustering troops, she gestured to the rest of the class, which, sensing conflict, perked up.

Mr Coates's face went as red as his tie and he held more firmly onto the Bible. Then he stepped out from behind the lectern and stuck out his chin. His voice was combative as he huffed, 'I'd suggest it's a courtesy at the very least and since you come from "over the water" (he made it sound like a contagious disease), you won't have lived with the problems of a divided country or realised the importance of unity in a working environment.'

There was a chilly silence broken by Margaret who stuck up her hand. She was sweetly reasonable and all for her own particular harmony.

'Well, I'm from the South. Strong Baptist, actually, so I can see the necessity of it – so of course I'll be taking it.' She stood up then advanced on the lectern with a winning smile. 'Now what do we do?'

'Oh well – I suppose if we must, we must,' said Cynthia with bad grace.

'We'll take you last,' the civil servant made a line of his mouth, 'so that you have plenty time to consider making this pledge.' This allowed Cynthia, short of a drum roll, to eventually make her pledge sound the loudest.

'He looks as if he could do with a big fart,' Seonaid muttered as, processing duties over, the man of God in government left, the Bible tucked under his arm giving him a righteous air.

We smothered a giggle whilst Matron, another tome to hand, was according it equal respect. Whilst her hands obliterated the author's name, the title in gold lettering was clear: *The Student Midwives' Guide to Midwifery.*

'I'd recommend you buy this textbook because it covers the first six-month part of your course and has all the necessary material for the exam which you'll have to pass before taking the second part.'

'The girls may have already bought the *Myles' Book of Midwifery,*' Miss Harvey said. 'It's very comprehensive, written by a Scots woman – an Aberdonian, in fact.

Matron looked her up and down before giving a disapproving sniff. 'Well, of course Aberdeen has a reputation in its own right.' Hostility was contained even if somewhere close a shillelagh and claymore might be readying for battle.

As well as having taken up half my luggage, the thick volume that lay on the desk before me had been recommended by *The Midwives' Almanac.* I hadn't properly looked at it, since the photographs of grim-looking nurses with hems trailing the ground were hardly page-turners. Added to that were graphic pictures of so many dire abnormalities in pregnancy and labour it would have had anybody demanding an early exit strategy and clamouring for contraception clinics. No wonder it wasn't on Matron's bookshelf.

I couldn't imagine or want any more information on the subject but the eagle-eyed

Margaret had spotted the author's name on the book Matron was promoting.

'Pardon me for asking, Matron, but would you have written this?'

'Since you ask, yes.' The coy response was a prospect every bit as alarming as the stern countenance befitting the keeper of Belfast's great unborn, but I wasn't fooled by the careless shrug. She wanted us to buy that book.

4

A SITE VISIT

'I presume someone's putting your name down for you to buy the book?' Matron asked as Seonaid, legs a blur, was leaving the lecture hall.

'Ach, no thanks. I'll buy it when I've the money. Now if you'll excuse me, I've a bit of an emergency.' She clutched her stomach, rolled her eyes, then sped off. For such a small person she left a big gap.

'Money management is one of the crucial aspects of operating professionally,' said Matron coldly, 'but if the rest of you want, you can put your names down now. Then you can be sure you'll get this book and have an appropriate reference right from the start.' She handed out a sheet of paper that we, drone like, signed.

'They'll be ready for you this afternoon. My secretary will bring them along. What's that nurse's name?'

Miss Harvey seemed to have gone deaf but we got the feeling that Seonaid's card was already marked. As Matron turned to go, Margaret put up her hand and said, 'It'd be nice to have your autograph.'

'Surely that'd spoil it,' whispered Marie, already checking in her purse. Margaret's ingratiating way had put my teeth on edge. 'Sook!' I muttered,

'What's a sook?' Marie wondered.

I was lofty. 'Somebody who sucks up to another person higher up, for personal gain.'

A bell with all the subtlety of a Klaxon rang as Matron, giving a gracious incline, left.

'That's a sign there's an imminent birth,' Miss Harvey explained. She rolled up her sleeves. 'You need to witness ten and have them recorded and attested in these books before you actually get any hands-on experience.' She started to hand out small jotters. 'If you open them you'll see there's other things that you'll need to witness as well as do, so we can be sure you're getting an all-round practical experience to match the theory.'

The list was formidable and seemed to include everything from breathing to brain surgery.

'Don't let it overwhelm you,' Miss Harvey advised. 'After all, you've a whole year to get through it. Ah, Nurse Fitzsimons.' Seonaid had returned, looking perky. 'You're just in time to collect your record book. Guard this one with your life.' She tapped it as if typing. 'There's no charge, but it's the most valuable possession you'll have. If you look inside you'll see there's places for signatures from trained staff verifying you've completed these tasks. Without this book and without the signatures, you won't be allowed to sit the finals.'

'Oh right!' Seonaid was sanguine as she took the book, tucking it carelessly under her arm. 'And did I miss anything else?'

'Only the year's bestseller. Now don't lose that one. Right! Let's get on.' Miss Harvey swivelled on her heel and pointed to the three words on the blackboard.

Intrigued, I leant forward, wondering what Cynthia and Margaret would make of them. With a bit of luck they'd have a punch-up over the 'attitude' one and ease the way to an early coffee break.

The tutor picked up a piece of chalk, holding it like a conductor's baton. 'It's amazing what babies get up to in the uterus,' she said and sketched a series of differently-shaped

44

balloons, 'considering the womb – ha ha!' With a sure hand, she drew a baby in each bubble, beguiling in activities ranging from frolics to resting in angelic slumber.

'After a little practice, you'll learn how to identify "Lie", "Attitude" and "Presentation". See – this is the best lie, attitude and presentation for a baby to be in before birth.' She pointed to a little haloed person, perfectly curled up in its bubble, head down and patiently queuing as if waiting for a show to start. 'Not like this.' She pointed to a party animal doing a moonie. 'Not a good way to present.' She put a cross over its bum sitting over the exit, 'Breech position! Wrong, babe. Wrong.' It sounded like a song.

'Right now,' she continued, 'impossible as it may seem, you're going to learn by observation and palpation,' her hand described a bread-making pummel, 'how a baby lies, and how easy its birth is going to be. Crystal gazing, it is not. No, it's the practice that's going to do it, and we'll make a start this morning after the coffee break when we go to the antenatal ward. Sister's got a couple of very different patients for us to see.'

The dining room was busy with staff crowding the long easy-wipe tables, some of which flanked a waterfall feature. It had the disconcerting habit of working intermittently.

'Makes it sound like a gents' toilet,' remarked Lorna as we queued at the self-service counter.

'Too right. Let's not go near it,' said Seonaid, loading up her tray with enough coffee and soda scones to feed an army. 'It'll make us all want to run at the same time.'

'That shouldn't worry you, you've just been,' I said. 'Anyway, it's where all the grandees are.' I nodded at a table full of white coats deep in conversation. 'They look just as self-important as our lot back in Aberdeen.'

One of the Belfast girls laughed, 'They're just the medical students and probably discussing the best place to drink Guinness.'

'Doesn't sound too healthy. Think I'll settle for fruit.' I smiled at the counter assistant.

'Pars?'

I looked around. Her look was direct and she was definitely speaking to me.

'Pars?' she repeated, beginning to sound exasperated and placing dumbbell arms on her hips. She was short and square and her name tag gave her the unlikely name of Daisy.

'Could ye make up yer mind? I haven't all day.'

'Come on, Janet, we haven't either. You're holding us all up. She's asking if you want a pear.' The speaker was a young chap queuing behind me. In contrast to his colleague with his jingling change and foxy furrowed face, he had an open, cheerful, relaxed way and leant his back on the counter, hands in his pockets.

Daisy sighed. 'Youse medical students have no patience. Just hold on, would ye.' She took a pear, dusted it on her overall then handed it over.

'Great.' I wished I'd the courage to ask for one less battle scarred.

'Grrrreat! Och aye the noo,' echoed both students, doubling up with mirth.

I could have said they were a right pair but only thought of it when back and following Miss Harvey now taking us into the hospital proper.

Smaller than Aberdeen's Foresterhill, Belfast's Royal Maternity felt like an antiseptic railway station where only a train arrival could bring excitement and galvanise the place into action. With its linoleum-grey floor menacing with glitter, the long corridor breathed carbolic whilst the odd notice broke up the putty-coloured walls with suitably improving health and visitor information notices. From a small corridor off the main one came the sound of clinking bottles.

'That's where the bottle feeds are made up,' said Miss Harvey. 'In the absence of any mother's home brew, it's our very own dairy.'

'But only supplying to babies, I hope, and where's the main entrance?' I asked, hoping it was a little more welcoming than the back-door one.

Miss Harvey said, 'It's one floor up beside the admission and waiting rooms and of course, as Matron made clear, her office.' From the cool inference she might have said 'dragon's den' before she continued, 'People get to the hospital from Grosvenor Road. It's just off the Falls Road.'

There were wards leading off at the far end whilst nearer was a windowed area looking over a narrow corridor into a glass-enclosed room.

'That's the Special Care Unit,' explained the tutor. We stared into another planet where paper-capped phantoms in white dresses tended to tiny babies in incubators.

Oblivious to all but the one wheeled in its little enclosed world to the corridor between there and the spectating window was a girl in a grubby quilted dressing gown. She gazed through the glass with the concentration of a child outside a sweetshop. As she secured her straggly hair into a ponytail she stood on heeled mules for a better view. She seemed too young to even tie up her own coat.

Enclosed in her bubble, the baby gasped with the stressed endeavour of a newly-landed fish. Occasionally her tiny limbs jerked. A thin feeding line threaded up one nostril and seemed like a gross intrusion on such a fragile existence. The sweetie pink card incongruously announced she was Mary-Jo Fleming. 3lbs. 1oz.

'Such a big name for a wee girl.' I was surprised my voice had gone husky, then was clutched by Marie as the girl suddenly froze and started knocking frantically on the window.

'She's stopped breathing!' she yelled. Her fingers scrabbled on the glass. 'Oh God! Somebody help her. Mother of God, please!' The cry was heart rending and resounded down that empty corridor where in the distance a baby cried as if in echo.

All bar Seonaid stopped, uncertain what to do whilst she floated to the young woman's side and took her arm. Miss Harvey had gone ahead but now came back looking puzzled, then pleased, as on the other side of the glass, a turquoise-dressed ball appeared, gently tapped the incubator like a discreet caller and prompted Mary-Jo to kick a leg as if in irritation at being disturbed.

'Good old Sister Bell, always keeping a lookout,' said Miss Harvey, noting our collective sigh of relief. 'Sometimes the premature babies need a wake-up call – they can be so far away they occasionally forget to breathe. She'd have been all right but Mum's had a fright, poor thing.'

She tapped the girl lightly on the shoulder. 'Look, my dear, Sister's signalling for you to see her in her office. See, there's the door, just down the corridor a bit and I'm sure she'll put your mind at rest. As for us,' she looked at her fob watch, 'we must press on. Antenatal awaits.'

Whoever had designed the ward entrance must have been anticipating either a hurricane, flood or sonic boom. The heavy doors had rubber sealing all the way round, including flaps at the bottom presumably to stop an incoming tide or maybe the noise of screams from the labour ward directly opposite.

From my ward maiding days, I recognised and saluted the hard work and polish spent on the brass handle on which Miss Harvey was now pushing and plainly not expecting the other half of the door to burst open. A burly man in a white coat barged through, practically flattening Cynthia who'd been trying to beat Miss Harvey to it.

'Mind out!' he snapped. With the look of a cross turkey cock he shook his wattles and strutted past. His splendour was somewhat dimmed by the following raggle taggle army of medical students, identifiable because my dining room irritants were there and winking as they followed.

'That's Professor McQuaid.' Miss Harvey's tone was dry. 'Always in a hurry.'

Margaret fluttered her eyelashes. 'My

surgeon, Jim, used to be a bit like that and sometimes I had to chivvy him a little when he got impatient.'

'My surgeons were always most courteous.' Cynthia was indignant. 'That man's very rude.'

'But not as rude as Nurse Macpherson sticking her tongue out at the students,' Miss Harvey observed. 'Now come along, class, we've work to do.'

5

AN ANTENATAL VISIT

Apart from a couple of women, everybody else was out of bed and being rounded up by a staff midwife in a gender-insensitive pink uniform. Sister Uprichard, labelled and unmissable in red, was handing out vitamin tablets like prizes in a ward that had the congenial atmosphere of a WI meeting where everybody's jam had set.

She had a kindly way, the rosy cheeks of a countrywoman and the manner of a jolly hostess. Slipping the bottle in her pocket she greeted Miss Harvey with enthusiasm. 'Top o' the morn! I've just been asking these girls if they'd like to be your guinea pigs,' she nodded at the two left in bed. They didn't look too happy.

'I expect you met the Prof.?' She slapped her battleship sides and sighed. 'I'm afraid he was a bit abrupt with them. You know how he can be.'

Miss Harvey cast her eyebrows and gave a laconic, 'True.' A word especially suited to a Scot's accent and making the Irish girls snigger.

Sister Uprichard continued, unperturbed. 'So I was delighted you and your rookies were coming. Youll be sure to make them feel useful as well as taking their minds off him saying they're lucky to be here.' She gave a vast chuckle gesturing at the ward's peeling plaster, faded curtains and drab lino. 'Lucky!'

Long windows gave out onto the blank walls of the general hospital, and from somewhere not far away, plumbing sounds emanated with a clank and splash. Yet, despite these dingy surroundings, the place was full of bright chat.

'Ach, Sister, you've got it like a holiday camp, it feels so free an' easy,' said one girl waving the air to let her nail varnish dry. 'I can't think why Staff's taking us away to relaxation classes when we could be enjoying the craic here.' In an exhaust of *California Poppy* scent, she joined the others, a fleet of tug boats chugging past.

'Better for me but up to you,' Sister said, starting to pull the curtains round the bed of our first patient. 'You'll be running soon enough. But be sure and come back. A wee bird told me some of you sneaked out the other night and came back the worse of the wear. It's no wonder we've confiscated your outdoor clothes. Locked them away until you're ready to go home.'

'Ah now, Sister, you wouldn't want to be depriving us of a bit of fun would ye?'

'Yes I would – especially if you didn't ask me to come along and chaperone you.'

The girl chuckled, 'A bit late for that!' and hurried to catch up with the others.

'Girls!' sighed Sister Uprichard and turned to a very young redhead. 'Now poor Mrs Campbell here's not thinking of going anywhere with her first baby making her a martyr to sickness. We've had to take her in to stop her from getting run down. A change of environment is meant to be part of the cure, but as you'll see she's taken a florist's shop with her.'

Apart from the chrome sickness bowl taking up space on her locker there were flowers crowded into every possible area, their splashes of colour in bright contrast to the girl's ashen face.

'My, but somebody must think you're special.' Miss Harvey nodded at a photograph stuck behind the sickness bowl. 'And

53

would that be your husband?'

The handsome fellow leaning against the tractor could have been an advertisement for toothpaste or the joys of agriculture.

The girl gave an indifferent shrug and a pout so eloquent I thought I might practise one like it as soon as I found a mirror.

'That's William. And he wouldn't be half as cheerful if he was having this baby.' She started to retch, tiny shrew-like hands blindly searching for the bowl just out of reach.

'Quick, Nurse Smythe, help her.'

Cynthia did, looking horrified as vomit splattered her apron whilst at the same time a doctor stuck his head round the screen.

'Sorry to bother you but d'you mind if I take some blood, Denise?'

He was tall with sleepy eyes which might have explained the lack of observational skills but Miss Harvey made him register with an irritated, 'This is definitely not a good time, Doctor, so if you want to do something really useful you could take Nurse Smythe here and show her where she can clean up.'

His gaze swung lazily round the group. 'Oh! Okey dokey. Sorry. Didn't mean to stop the progress of medical science. Uh, I'll catch you later, Denise.' He returned his head and Cynthia followed him at a rate bordering on trot. I handed tissues to Denise who seemed to have perked up. This doctor's visit was obviously a healthier option than ours.

'That Dr Welch's a lovely man.' Denise twiddled an auburn ringlet then laid it carefully on a shoulder, thin as a chicken wing. 'He's so sympathetic about me having all this pregnancy trouble, you'd never credit he's a single fella himself and when he takes off blood you wouldn't ever know there was a needle there.' For a moment, she was almost enthusiastic.

'That's good,' said Miss Harvey in an unimpressed way and advanced, rubbing her hands. 'And it's even better that you're allowing these budding midwives loose on that tummy of yours and, may I just say, what a neat one it is.'

Denise rolled her eyes, slid down the bed and bared her stomach. 'I think it's gross but help yourselves.'

We craned round like avid telly watchers whilst Miss Harvey got hearty. 'What nonsense! Look, class, a perfect shape. And just think, Mrs Campbell, when you're as old as me you can tell your grandchildren how you played a big part in the future careers of a group of students.'

'It'll be bad enough being a mother,' said Denise, refusing to be cheered. 'I don't know how I'll cope.'

Her eyes wandered the ceiling as if searching for an exit strategy and she spoke as if she had detached herself from her body, which seemed an incredible feat given so much going on inside it.

'Lovely! And look! The baby's lying in a perfect position too. I can feel its spine right here.' Miss Harvey placed her hand on one side of the baby bump and pushed whilst her fingers played along the other in an exploratory way. 'Perfect! Ah, splendid! Lying just how it should be! And right here above the supra pubic area you can feel Junior's head.' Miss Harvey's pincer-like grasp seemed unduly firm and rather personal, and when she started wriggling her hand in a pendulum moving way, I expected Denise to protest but she merely gave a bored yawn.

The tutor took a metal instrument shaped like an old-fashioned bicycle horn from her pocket. 'This is a foetal stethoscope and it's for hearing the baby's heart.' She placed the trumpet-shaped bit on Denise's belly and listened at the other end with the concentration of an eavesdropping telephonist.

'Excellent.' She gave an approving nod. 'Doing nicely, thank you, and happy for the class to listen in. Come along, Nurse Macpherson, see what you can hear.'

I took the stethoscope, aimed for the spot recently vacated and tuned in. It was like a radio station with interference. Denise on the outside might be comatose but she'd plenty action inside. I listened harder, then over food-processing noises, came, like hurrying footsteps, the sound of quick regular beats. Either Denise had swallowed a time bomb or I was hearing a baby's heart.

Seeing my surprised and pleased look, Miss Harvey said, 'Right! Now see if you can find the baby's head.'

Imitating Miss Harvey's grasp and reminded of a lucky dip, I foraged and at last found a ball-like shape.

'Amazing!' was the best I could do but must have looked enthused enough for the class to move forward, anxious to have a go.

'It might be harder to find the spine. See what you can do.'

I tried but only found small knobbly lumps.

'Hey, Denise! You've certainly got a mixed bag in there.' I bent down to level with her, trying to engage her interest. 'Mind you, I'd a bit of a job understanding your baby's Irish accent.'

But Denise refused to be patronised. 'You try having one and see how jokey that makes you,' she said and gave a cold stare to Marie who had been handed the stethoscope and was now approaching with a trembling hand and her eyes already swimming. A sob hovered.

She gazed into Denise's face.

'Well if I was in your place, I'd be sick too,

but with nerves.'

'Oh for goodness sake!' Miss Harvey threw her eyes heavenward. 'A birth's supposed to be a cause for joy. Put your ear to that stethoscope and see if you can hear something positive for a change.'

But further negativity came from outside with Sister's voice carrying a cool, hostile message.

'No, Father, I'm very much afraid you can't visit Mrs Murphy. She's very kindly agreed to help Miss Harvey with her tutorial and that's about to start right now.' She turned up the volume. 'Right now! Isn't that so, Miss Harvey?'

'Ach, Sister, I just want a wee word with Mrs Murphy. She's one of my flock and I'm here to wish her well.' The tone was wheedling.

'Well, we'll pass on your best wishes,' Miss Harvey broke in. Quickly she grabbed the stethoscope, returned Denise's bump to its owner, swished back the curtains and looked at her watch. 'Heavens! Is that the time? You'll have to excuse us, Mrs Campbell. My! How the time does fly. Our next patient must be thinking we've forgotten her. Come along, class.' She hustled us out past a priest who was facing up to an unexpectedly implacable Sister Uprichard.

His round figure, halo of wispy curls and rosebud mouth in its florid setting gave him the look of a dissolute cherub but he wore the certainty of a God-messenger on a mission.

'Well, if it's not Miss Harvey, me oulde friend.' He couldn't have sounded less delighted. 'Look,' he ran a finger round a grimy dog collar, 'I'll only take a minute. She's one of our most dearly beloved flock.' He clasped his hands and gazed at the floor as if already praying. 'And the baby being so near and all, I have a special wee word for her.'

'I'm sure God, like us, is busy enough right now and as we don't know how long we're going to be, I suggest that a better use of your time would be to visit the Murphy family in their home. Offer help. There must be at least nine hungry mouths to feed there, Father.' Miss Harvey spoke pleasantly whilst making it clear the subject was closed. Going to Mrs Murphy's bed she started to screen her off. 'Come along, class, we've work to do.'

Released from the doubtful pleasures of abdominal palpation, Denise wondered where Dr Welch was. Cynthia, who had returned looking smug, bustled off again, saying she knew where to find him. Her apron had been rinsed clean but also of starch. Now it drooped like a sad flag. It made her look more human if less efficient.

Meanwhile the priest hovered, reluctant to

leave. Miss Harvey, hands on the curtains, waited until Sister Uprichard took his arm and, propelling him towards the door, spoke with the hearty manner of a hostess seeing off her last and least welcome guest. 'Now, Father, I'll see you out and maybe when this Baby Murphy's born you can run along and give Mum a hand, hang out the nappies. There'll be plenty of them already. I imagine the last little Murphy's still in them.'

She opened the door and he trudged off whilst we gathered round Mrs Murphy who, unlike Denise, on whose small finger a large gem had sparkled, wore a wedding ring strung by a shoelace round her neck. Her swollen fingers busied themselves knitting whilst she kept a watchful eye on her new visitors.

We didn't need to be experts to figure out that this patient with the care-worn look of an all-day shopper, only able to afford shoddy goods for needy kids, was no first-time mother. Still, there was something about her direct gaze and carefully darned cardigan which commanded respect and suggested she was no pushover.

She sighed as she laid her knitting with its Bestway pattern to the side. 'I hope yez won't be too long – I'm wanting to get this vest finished today and I'm vexed ye sent Father O'Patrick away. He's a lovely man,' her tone was as protective as the arms she was placing over her stomach, 'and I'd have liked to have seen him. He always cheers me up and prays for me to be a good Mammy, but,' she looked down on a belly, its elasticity lost to pregnancy, and sighed, 'I don't suppose he'd have liked to see this.'

Miss Harvey was brisk. 'Nonsense! It'd have done him good. But what's really far more important is you allowing *us* to see you. It's vital these girls see lots of different tummies. We can't really thank you enough for helping. I'm sure Father would bless you for that alone.'

'And do you think that with all this education you could do something with these?' Mrs Murphy pulled on greying hair and stuck out a well-travelled leg. 'With the varicose veins an' all?'

'We could suggest ways to stop you getting more.'

'Every babby's a blessing,' Mrs Murphy bridled. 'And sure my husband wouldn't approve.'

Miss Harvey was thoughtful. 'You could always take matters in your own hands.' She dropped her voice and said as discreetly as you could in front of a class of suddenly attentive students, 'What would you think about a Dutch cap?'

If anybody had missed the conversation they were quickly brought up to speed as Mrs Murphy's scandalised words rang out through the ward. 'Cap? Cap!' She drew breath, then exploded, 'Sure the only cap me man would wear is on his head.'

A heavy silence fell, broken by Lorna who, picking up the pattern, said it was a bargain at three pence but probably not as good as the more comprehensive ninepenny Patons and Baldwin. For a glorious moment I thought she was going to suggest it might even have a pattern for contraception and maybe Lorna, with her kindly way, might knit one up for her.

'Thank you, Nurse.' Miss Harvey had the unfazed manner of a bombproof head mistress. 'I can see you'll be good at mother craft lessons but maybe we should have a chat with our patient about family planning later.' She put her hands together in a poor imitation of Father O'Patrick's prayerful way. 'But we're actually here because of her unstable lie. You girls need to see one to recognise it.'

There was another silence even louder than the last as the patient looked at her in amazement. Then she sat bolt upright, her lined face flushed whilst she jabbed with a finger. 'First you stop me seeing my priest, then you've some yarn about hats and now you're saying I've an unstable eye. Well, that's it! I'll thank you for taking that back. I don't know when I was so insulted. Mother of God!' She blinked hard. 'See? Straight!

And I'll have you know there's nothing wrong with my eyesight either. I'm here because the babby isn't in a good position,' she flung back the bed clothes, 'but I'm not staying here to have you speak to me like this. Where's me clothes?' Those hard-working fingers scrabbled with the buttons of her cardigan.

Miss Harvey sucked her lips as if regretting her words and quickly laid a smoothing hand on her shoulder. 'I'm sorry. I've really upset you and I'm the one forever telling the students not to frighten their patients with medical jargon. Forgive me. I got it wrong.' She closed her eyes and tapped her head twice. 'Look! Maybe these rookies will do a better job.' She glanced down at Seonaid practising small skips at the bottom of the bed. 'So what could I have said to our patient without giving her a heart attack?'

Mrs Murphy's bump was getting in the way so Seonaid had to tiptoe to let Mrs Murphy see her,

'I'd say, m'dear, you've a rock'n'roll chick in there takin' up all the floor an' dancin' everywhere – groovin' about an' sometimes even falling asleep over the door. That's some wee mover you've got in there, so you have. All over the place now.' Seonaid clicked her fingers and swivelled her hips as if getting into the beat herself.

'No, I wouldn't have thought of saying

that,' Miss Harvey mused whilst a young girl sneaked out from behind Mrs Murphy's worry lines.

Lying back on her pillow she said, 'But sure, that's clear enough and rock'n'roll's gas but,' she sighed, putting a hand wearily over her brow, 'this mammy won't be doing it for a while.'

Miss Harvey resumed her tutorial.

'And certainly not until Junior's born. Wouldn't be too good for your blood pressure but if you do go into labour, at least here there's medical help right at hand. And why do you think she might need that, class?'

Margaret's theatre experience of dealing with unconscious patients had plainly affected her communication skills as she said, 'The wrong bit might come out first, leaving the rest to get stuck.'

'Oh!'

I thought it was a Marie response but it was Mrs Murphy who, in an affronted way, had lifted the bedclothes, peered down then bulked herself into a different position.

'Me bags have burst!' she said.

6

AN UNEXPECTED ARRIVAL

Even if the placid pace of the antenatal ward quickened, Miss Harvey was calm. 'Well, what a good thing you're in here. It's so easy to get you into labour ward.' Signalling for us to do likewise, she kicked off the nearest brakes on the bed and started to shove it. 'We'll just pop you over the road.'

'Mrs Murphy's membranes have ruptured,' she said as we passed Sister Uprichard guarding the door, presumably to keep good priests out and her fun-loving girls back in. 'We'll take her, and it's a chance to show the class the labour suite as well. Come on, folks, let's help this lady on her way!' She gave a little chuckle. 'My! But this is turning out to be a grand tour.'

We arrived in a tumble in the labour ward with Cynthia and Margaret making the bed swerve from side to side as they fought for front rider supremacy, the rest of us hanging on like flanking troops.

'I see you've brought Mrs Murphy over and by the look of you, taking in more than one unstable lie,' said a doctor applying midwifery terms to our driving skills. He led our zig-zag procession to a small cell-like room. He was tall with the easy way good-looking doctors seem to have of establishing trust and co-operation from everybody but those with sight impairment. His sleeves, rolled up in a workmanlike fashion, showed forearms so brown he must either take holidays abroad or be an axe man. He swept back a lock of fair hair as if to see the better for checking any damage. 'I just hope you haven't chipped the door of our Labour Suite.'

Suite! What a misnomer for a cold clinical collection of rooms with walls the colour of puce and the floor a cheerless swabbed-down grey. Each labour room was bare, the soundproof door completing its cell-like image. I thought it a particularly dismal place to be born and a doctor, no matter how handsome, should care less for the paintwork and more for his patient, even if she didn't seem bothered.

In fact, Mrs Murphy was wreathed in smiles. 'I've had all my babbies here and had the best of treatment so I know I'm in good hands, and of course Dr O'Reilly here always looks after me great. My first time, d'you remember, you were just a student-doctor and look at you now.' She clapped her hands and widened her smile. 'An obstetrician, no less. So I couldn't have put you off or been too bad a patient.' She sank her head back on the pillow and looked at him in a dreamy way.

'You've never been that and of course we're old friends and we'll not let you down this time either,' promised the doctor. He might have looked like a film star but he wasn't above meeting his public and he seemed cheerful and especially pleased to see this most regular of patients. 'But maybe having them doesn't get any easier.'

With the authority of a judge summoning his clerk, he beckoned on a nearby pretty blonde nurse. 'Staff here'll make sure everything's in order. I presume you've signed the anaesthetic forms?'

'Now why would I need to do that?'

The door closed on us and the answer. It plainly disappointed Margaret who, breathless with excitement, was eyeing up the theatre like a circus horse smelling sawdust.

'Miss Harvey, do you think Mrs Murphy'll need a Caesarean?'

'If the baby can't be turned, yes, but Dr O'Reilly's very experienced and should manage to get that baby on course. It's no surprise, and with all that muscle stretch, she's bound to have a quick labour so he'll need to be snappy. Right now that baby's in a transverse lie.'

'It'd be good to get a normal delivery for a start,' I said, not wanting to see Mrs Murphy under the knife and thinking that the combination of Cynthia and Margaret in theatre presented more hazards than any scalpel.

'Well, we'll ask Sister Flynn if there's any likely. She's in charge, and'll know.' Miss Harvey nodded at a sister in theatre-green charging towards us.

Unlike Sister Uprichard, she was whippet thin, with a beaky nose and the harried expression of someone with more important things to do than stop.

'She looks desperate strict. I bet she gives terrible rows,' whispered Marie, tucking in behind Margaret and plucking my arm, 'and, Jane, if we do see a delivery should we not have our record books?'

'We've a primigravida in room five.' Sister Flynn, skidding to a halt, nodded her head backwards. 'Shouldn't be long, but we'll need to ask if she minds an audience. It's her first time, after all. Anyway, I don't want too many in at one time and the Prof.'s kicking up because his students are leaving soon and still haven't witnessed all their births never mind getting their deliveries.' She grimaced as if she was part of an inefficient postal service.

Miss Harvey was in the nice mode we were coming to associate with the opposite. 'Well, we're here and there's not that many of us, so why not just let us in and Prof. can have the next one? I'm sure he wouldn't mind. Anyway, we saw him leading his students away from here. Maybe he was going to give them a lecture.'

Sister Flynn rubbed her brow and scrubbed her paper cap, putting it at an angle that could have made her look jolly were it not for the beady eyes. 'I'm sure he will mind, but you are here I suppose and these nurses will need their witnessing too even if they have a whole year compared to the students' three months.'

'Yes but my nurses'll be midwives at the end of it.' Miss Harvey sounded edgy. 'And of course unless a medic chooses midwifery as a specialism, they're unlikely to be practising it when they've qualified.'

'Well, of course I know that.' Sister Flynn, practically running on the spot, was making the point about being a very busy person without time to argue. 'OK then, but you'll need to go along and ask her. I'm far too busy. I need to check that everything's ready in theatre just in case we need it for that new patient you've brought in.' She sounded faintly accusing.

'Right, I'll go and, class, mind you don't get in anybody's way,' said Miss Harvey and disappeared in the direction of Sister Flynn's nod.

She'd no sooner gone than the professor stuck his head round the entrance doors.

'Any deliveries likely?' Even though he'd a

mouth like a trap door, he sounded civil, unlike Cynthia who, as self-appointed spokesperson, spat a 'No' before pointedly turning her back on him and studying the ceiling with fierce determination.

The door banged shut. Miss Harvey was back, giving us no time to think guilt by association,

'I didn't hear Prof. McQuaid did I?'

Apart from Marie who looked shocked, the rest of us, determining to keep our witness slot, threw in our lot with Cynthia with a universal 'No.' Even Margaret joined the chorus.

Marie, a red spot on each cheek, bowed her head as Miss Harvey said, 'Funny, I was sure I heard his voice. I wouldn't like him to think we were stealing a march on his students. I know he's chasing witness deliveries at the moment but that's fine. We'll not bother with the "delivery notice" bell. Our patient's got a staff midwife and student in with her already but she says she doesn't mind a few more.'

'And she doesn't mind an audience?' Lorna asked.

Miss Harvey laughed. 'Says I can sell the tickets and she'll take the money. She shouldn't be long but if you go ahead into the delivery room it'll give you the chance to look round. I'll be with you in a moment.'

'Good,' said Cynthia, leading the way.

'One feels that preparation's everything.'

'Does one indeed,' I parodied, nevertheless falling into line and into a room where a huge wall clock, scales, cot, delivery table and enough sanitary ware to mop up Belfast Lough, made for dull props in the silent theatre that was the delivery room.

Half the wall at the far end was windowed in frosted glass. Sunlight filtered through it. As if it were a warm-up performance, it played on the chrome instruments that were laid on a trolley like cutlery, giving a brighter lighting effect than the spotlighting disc hanging from the ceiling and trained on the bottom of the delivery table.

'Looks as if it's waiting for the star attraction and what's that blue machine at the top?' I wondered.

'Ah! Now that's an easy one.' Margaret stepped forward, relishing the role of mystery object advisor. Dropping shoulders, stretching her neck and jutting her formidable chin, she stood beside the machine with the air of a salesperson promoting a good product. 'D'you see the cylinders? That's Entonox, or gas and air if you'd prefer.' She held up a mask and held it close to her face.

'If you take that any nearer, you'll have to clean it before anybody else uses it,' Cynthia observed.

Margaret glared at her. 'From the way you're talking, you'd think I'd a notifiable disease. Of course I wasn't going to use it. I just wanted to demonstrate that you can't overdose on it. The patient holds it like so.' Defying Cynthia with a closeness that made me think she was actually going to take a quick snort, Margaret put the mask in front of her again. 'It helps take the edge off pain but also'll leave her in control which might not seem too apparent at the moment.' She cupped her ear. 'Listen! Here she comes.'

Followed by Miss Harvey, our patient arrived threshing about in a bed wheeled in by a student and Staff Midwife.

Miss Harvey made the introductions. 'This is Jinty Allan, and she's a very brave girl.'

'No I'm not. I need help. I'm in agony. Help! When's all this going to stop? Oh Jasus!'

Jinty's name was the most cheerful thing about our patient. The sinews of her neck stuck out like whipcord, sweat stuck her curly hair to her forehead in dark question marks whilst her knees seemed to have relocated to her chin. She ground her teeth and groaned. 'It's purgatory. I'll never do this again. Never!'

'That's what they all say,' said the midwife, 'but it is hard work and you've been doing so well. Won't be long now.' She moved over to the table, patting it in an encouraging way. 'Now! Between your pains could you move onto this?'

Had anybody suggested I climb the north face of a delivery table from an existing bed of pain I'd have refused, but our patient was apparently made of sterner stuff and heroically scaled the heights before making her crash landing. Another yell split the air.

'Mother of God. Another bed of misery!'

'Have this. It should help,' said Margaret handing her the Entonox which Jinty grabbed, inhaling with the enthusiasm of a smoker on a forty-a-day habit.

'I'm conducting this delivery,' snapped the midwife, 'and you're supposed to be just watching. Go down and join the others please and mind out for the student midwife coming towards you. She's scrubbed up, ready to do the delivery.'

'You'll see better from here. It's better than a ringside seat,' I whispered, making room for a crimson-faced Margaret.

'I was only trying to help,' she muttered and looked close to tears.

'Well see if you can get Marie to open her eyes, otherwise she'll miss this delivery. She trusts you for some reason.'

Having made sure her class was still in the upright position, if a little green, Miss Harvey murmured that she was going back to the classroom. 'And, class, I'll see you there after. And the best of luck, Mrs Allan, you're going to be fine.'

'If anybody else says that I'll scream,' gritted our patient and did.

'Oh, good. Transition stage and I think we can just see the head.' The midwife sounded positively breezy. 'Now mind how you control it, Nurse. We don't want it shooting out.'

It was one thing having an audience for your labour but there was the student mid-wife's performance too to consider. I wondered if she felt nervous about us watching or did she know our attention was as solely glued to her baby-catching hand as it was to the emerging head.

'Pant!' yelled the midwife.

'Not you,' I nudged Marie.

'She's hyperventilating,' excused Margaret, 'but for goodness sake, Marie, let go of my hand.'

'We've lied, we've lied,' whimpered Marie, 'and now this!'

Under cover of Mrs Allan's impression of a dog expiring in the sun, the midwife picked up scythe-sized scissors and said, 'She's going to need an episiotomy – otherwise she'll tear.'

I had to take that deep breath forbidden to Jinty and wondered if I really wanted to be a midwife. Blood sports had nothing on this. Maybe life behind a nice tidy desk in a smart office was the way forward where the nearest thing to drama was the phone ringing. Still, I forced myself to watch, holding my breath as the scissors made a quick cut. The sound of metal on flesh was toe-curling.

I supposed that a surgical cut to make an easier passage for the baby would make a clean wound. It would be easier to heal. Even then, it might be a while before Jinty could sit without discomfort.

Somewhere, outside, was a simple world where people happily went about their business. They'd have no anxieties like those delivering new lives, here, in this clinical space. Never mind midwifery, I vowed, I'll make damn sure I'll skip motherhood.

Then, almost as an anticlimax, the baby's head was eased out.

'Another wee push now.'

Shoulders emerged and then the rest of the baby. The cord was cut, airways briskly cleared and cleaned, and the baby wrapped in a cloth. Then, releasing the tension, a tiny cry made a loud statement.

'It's a girl! You've got a wee girl!' The student, sounding more excited than the mother, handed her over.

Jinty, weary and cradling the baby awkwardly, touched her cheek. 'A daughter!'

She sighed as she checked to see if the student was right. Then, with her vocal cords apparently affecting her as much as motherhood, she said in a voice like broken glass, 'Ah ye poor wee thing. You're crying now but you don't know what lies ahead of ye.'

7

'WHERE THERE IS WHISPERING THERE IS LYING.'

'That left nothing to the imagination,' said Seonaid, allowing the labour ward suite door to swing shut behind us. 'And to think Mrs Murphy's gone through it nine times already. The woman needs a medal for endurance!' She shook her head. 'Or a new brain.'

Passing the theatre door on our way out, we'd seen a red light above it. It was a sign that an operation was in progress. It must be for Mrs Murphy.

As impressed at so recently having being present at a birth as depressed by the perils of having so many, I said, 'Well something needs sorted. She must have had to have that Caesarean. I hope she's all right and maybe she'll get her tubes tied as well. Save a next time.'

'They'd need to get her husband's permission for that.' Margaret, probably rankling after getting that gas and air row, spoke with the authority of somebody bulked of it. 'It might be alright in Aberdeen but they do things differently here.'

'I'll take that as a compliment.' I was more aggravated than certain. Sterilisation wasn't a subject I remembered anything about but surely it couldn't be the case back home. If I'd thought the matter of stopping pregnancies by a simple enough operation was such a contentious subject I'd have paid more attention to the snooze-inducing lectures by droning old gynaecologists.

'Ah, girls, stop your arguing. Why don't you start praying for her like me?' Marie's colour was as retrieved as her faith.

Remembering some publicity about a burly, ugly-faced Ulster preacher coming to Aberdeen, I was exasperated. 'For the love of Mike, give that God of yours a break. When I was in Aberdeen we never bothered ours except maybe on a Sunday and then for just an hour.' I warmed to my theme. 'Then someone from Ireland came to preach in a well-loved church to,' I air-punctuated the words, '"*show us the way*". Apparently all he did was upset congregations and keep them awake by thundering a Hell, Fire and Damnation sermon. Then some large men put round pails to be filled with money, preferably notes, as a mark of gratitude.'

I chuckled. 'He must've forgotten he was

dealing with Aberdonians. The good folk had never seen or heard the like before and found his buckets and bigotry a complete turn off.'

Marie gave a horrified squeak. 'I'm sure that man wouldn't have been one of ours. I couldn't imagine any of them carrying a pail, but Jane,' her eyes were filled with anxiety, 'have you no worries about your soul?'

'Not really, but if it's worrying you and you're on the line to your God you can put in a word for me. Personally I think he's a bit overstaffed.' I nodded at Father O'Patrick heading our way. 'Look, just what I'm saying. Here's one of his busiest helpers.'

The priest blocked our path. 'Bless you, bless you! Just a minute of your time, if you don't mind. I know how busy you are but what I'm wondering is if you could ever tell me about Mrs Murphy. I happened to notice her being taken in there.' He pointed at the labour rooms whilst darting his eyes at the antenatal room doors with an anxiety which suggested a vision of Sister Uprichard wouldn't constitute a miracle.

'You mean the labour ward?' I asked, feeling bold at introducing a word that suggested hard work.

The priest nodded and scratched his curls, prompting an early fall of dandruff to snowstorm the black coat swaddled about him. It had a torn pocket from which a *Racing Times*

78

hung out lending cheer to the cold weather front of his person. 'I'm betting her husband will want to know she's there but as he hasn't a phone, I could tell him where she is and I could easily go now.'

'My good man, we couldn't possibly tell you anything about any patient,' said Cynthia, her chest advancing, 'that would be a terrible breach of confidentiality.'

Despite a position of vulnerability, trapped as he was under the shelf of Cynthia's bosom, Father O'Patrick fought back. Patting his *Racing Times* as if to reassure himself that better things lay ahead he said, 'But my dear girl, you won't know the family circumstances like I do, and believe me, Mr Murphy may well need my support right now.'

Cynthia's bosom continued inexorably as she said, 'We're not at liberty to disclose anything.'

Margaret, keen to put in her tuppence worth, hardened her jaw as she said, 'Professionalism comes in many shapes.'

I hadn't thought either Cynthia's chest or Margaret's chin fitted that category but they were doing their bit when Dr O'Reilly, looking harassed, barged through the labour ward doors.

'Ah! Father – that's a bit of luck. I was just nipping over to see Sister Uprichard to see how to contact Mr Murphy and she said you were probably still around. Mrs

Murphy's just had her baby and I need to contact him right away but we're having a problem getting a hold of him. Would you know if he has a telephone now?'

The priest gave us a smug 'told you so' look before thanking God for deliverance and the presence of a diligent messenger at such a crucial time.

'I know he doesn't have one but what is it and what will I tell him?'

The doctor looked solemn. 'I can't actually say but just let him know that the sooner I see him the better it'll be for everybody. Now, do you think you could go, and quickly too?'

'Well if you're sure I can't pass on any other message,' the priest said, looking cheated then frustrated. Then clutching at a straw, 'I've actually a few things to do here first so if you could tell me more…'

Horns could have locked had Seonaid not stepped forward and asked if the family lived nearby. Dr O'Reilly had to look down to locate the voice whilst the priest seemed relieved to find somebody with long sooty eyelashes and small enough to hardly pose any threat. 'Number Seventy-Six. It's just a wee way down the Falls Road, but it'll be no trouble for me to go, especially if it's an emergency.' Curiosity sharpened his tone. 'Look, I can do me other chores here later.'

'Ah! But I could easily run down just now,

and as you say you've work to do here. See, Father, I'm really fast,' Seonaid wiggled a shoe as if it had spikes. 'It'll be our lunch hour soon and I'm sure Miss Harvey won't mind. She knows Mrs Murphy.'

Dr O'Reilly brightened. 'That'd be even better. As you say, Father, you're a busy man and you've just said you've other things to do so maybe this nurse should go and she can check everything's alright in the household as well.' His eyes drifted over the priest's gravy stains whilst he added gently, 'And maybe you might not be the best judge of that.'

The priest looked thwarted then blue as a fit of coughing worthy of medical attention took over, giving Dr O'Reilly a perfect opportunity to hurry back to the real work of the labour ward.

As the priest recovered, his chin settled back into its pillow of Brillo-coloured jowl and he sighed. 'Ah, but these doctors all think they know best and, forgive me for saying so, but Miss Harvey may have her job to do whilst mine is a calling.' He made the comparison sound as if he was a hot-blooded saviour. 'You know the family is very special to me so I'll just hurry with my other tasks and follow you on then, Nurse.' But Seonaid was already out of negotiating range.

'Does that not remind you of a Christmas pudding on the run?' said Laura, nodding as the priest bobbed off in the opposite direction. 'But I suppose we should head back to the lecture room – Miss Harvey'll be waiting for us.'

As we passed the nursery Marie said, 'They must have allowed in Mammy Fleming. See? I'd know her by her hair. Ah, the wee love, she'll feel better being there and so much closer.' She pointed to a gowned figure under whose cap a ratty tail escaped and who was now gazing into Mary-Jo's incubator.

As unaware of us as her daughter was of her, the figure sat motionless, looking in with the same intensity as Marie whilst I hurried to catch up with Seonaid.

'I think the doctor wants Mrs Murphy to be sterilised, tubes tied and all that.'

'And I think her husband will too,' Seonaid cranked up her pace, 'once I've had a word with him, but I'll have to shift, Father O'Patrick's going to be right on my tail and I don't want him trailing in clouds of conscience and talk of God's will before I get my oar in.' As she sprinted past the lecture room she called back, 'Could you just tell Miss Harvey where I've gone.'

I wasn't sure if that was a good idea, especially as Miss Harvey nodded us in with a grin so fierce you might have thought she was my aunt welcoming an unexpected busload of hungry relations. Suddenly, I wished I'd gone with Seonaid.

'I want you all in and in your seats now!'

She slammed the door shut and leant against it as if we might escape, which I now very much wanted to do. There was a brief silence whilst she contemplated her shoes which were Edinburgh sensible, highly-polished and apparently a brighter sight than her class. Silence prevailed, then in a very cold voice she said, 'I've just had a visit from Professor McQuaid who'd come to fix up a time for a lecture I'd asked him to give. He was surprised nobody was here and when I told him where you actually were he said he'd been to the labour ward and was told there was nothing happening.'

Her sigh was as gusty as that of a chief mourner fighting against sleet. 'And I can tell you right now, he's just furious and for that matter so am I. He's a busy man and accustomed to respect. I believe he almost had a door shut in his face and then...' In an 'Outraged of Morningside' voice, she registered a far more serious crime. 'You lied to me as well. I want you all to know you've put me in a very embarrassing position. Against all my principles, I've had to defend you and say it was just you were so mustard keen to see an actual delivery you forgot yourselves.'

Even if she didn't appear to have noticed Seonaid's absence, perhaps this was not the time to explain it. The St Andrew's flags on

Margaret and Cynthia's backs flapped disconsolately whilst Miss Harvey stomped over to a shelf. 'And covering up for liars is not what I joined this profession to do.'

Having successfully laid a mantle of gloom and continuing the spirit of despondency, Miss Harvey picked up a decayed looking pelvis and the head of a doll so battered it merited social work intervention or an autopsy. With the care of an antique dealer happening on a rare find, she held up both artefacts. 'These are the Professor's and he uses them for his lecture on the Mechanism of Labour – his special subject.'

Mechanics and labour weren't words I could imagine putting together until Miss Harvey held the pelvis in one hand. With the other she put the doll's head through, turning it as if screwing a jar top,

'He uses this to demonstrate the different positions and action of a baby going head first during labour. Even though that's the best way, it can still deliver in lots of different ways. It's not always easy to grasp but it's fundamental to understanding those differences. Nobody explains it better than the Professor. We're privileged he's always done it for the student midwives. Now I'm not so sure...'

My head was beginning to spin at the same speed as the doll's, except it didn't have a body to worry about. I'd my stomach to consider. Surely a cancelled lunchtime wasn't on the cards. My mind drifted off to Seonaid and wandered back in time to catch Miss Harvey's winding-up lecture.

'I've assured the Professor that you won't be credited with witnessing that last delivery and that's helped a bit. Certainly seemed to cheer him up.' She gave a grim smile. 'So hopefully, and in a little while, he'll have calmed down and will come and give his lecture. Otherwise we'll all be wasting each other's time. I happen to value mine so whilst you're having lunch, think what you should profitably do with yours.'

8

A NIGHT ON THE TOWN

'Well, anyway, that's our first day over and we haven't killed anybody,' I said, 'but you should have let me speak up for you. I wouldn't have minded and I'm sure Miss Harvey'd have believed me. She might have been glad that at least one of us wasn't a liar.'

Marie only clutched her record book as if it might be snatched from her. 'Miss Harvey must think we're awful. What a way to start.

We'll be lucky if we're not kicked out.'

As we got out of the lift I determined to be cheerful. 'Just look on the bright side. See how you've forgotten your vertigo; here we are, right on top of the world; and think of all the lovely views from your room and how lucky you are to have the best one.'

Our corridor was as warm and welcoming as the maternity's wasn't with nurses in rollers sprawled over chairs in chatty groups. Untrammelled by parenthood cares, they were discussing ways to avoid them with dancing all night at Maxims' as good a way as any.

'And tonight should be great craic with the Showband there,' someone said, making me want to join the conversation. But I was with Marie and she was still set on a martyr's course.

'I wouldn't have wanted you getting into more trouble. Miss Harvey would just have said my principles should have made me speak up there and then.' Marie gnawed her knuckle and blinked hard. 'I'm such a coward. I shouldn't have been frightened to speak to the Professor.'

'And when you were squashed flat, given a posthumous medal for bravery? No! I suspect Miss Harvey would really have understood why you didn't say anything at the actual time.'

Marie looked doubtful and turned the key

in her lock. 'Ah, Jane, much as you're trying now, you're not making me feel any better.' She considered the middle distance. 'But confession now, that might – and there's a church nearby.'

'Confession? Confession! You've only been here five minutes and already you're a beacon of hope in a class of sinners.'

'No I'm not. I'm a sinner too.' She was determined on suffering.

'How come?'

She looked around very carefully, then drawing her head near mine, whispered, 'I've said flip three times.' She searched my face, obviously waiting for shock to register, then as the silence between us stretched, added. 'So now you must see why I need to go.'

'By Jove, yes,' I said, thinking, one up to you, God. Your little angel might faint if suggesting the Showband might be a better fix as well as helping us celebrate Seonaid's visit to Mr Murphy.

She'd returned when we'd been having lunch, breathless but triumphant.

'Just a dawdle,' she'd reported. 'I was cool as a breeze with the da. I think he was more stressed out about having his mother-in-law helping than hanging out nappies in his garden where he'd gone to escape. When I told him the Doc. needed to see him he asked why, so I said I didn't rightly know but maybe he should think about knot tying one way or another. He gave the washing line a good jiggle and said there was nothing wrong with it, and then Father Murphy arrived so I had to be quick.' Seonaid mimicked the trouser-hitching part of 'The Sailor's Hornpipe' then clapped her hands. 'He got that message alright.'

Marie gazed at her, round-eyed.

'You don't mean he should,' she dropped her gaze to her lap then faltered, 'get done.'

'A first for Belfast, I imagine,' I said dryly. 'Now you know why the Scots wear sporrans, Marie.'

'Ach! Would you stop your teasing, Jane?' Seonaid rebuked. 'At least Mr Murphy got something other than the washing to think about. Father O'Patrick tried for a word but I told him we mustn't mess with Dr O'Reilly's time, and if Mr Murphy came now I could get him in by the back entrance so's it'd be quicker.'

'And what about Father O'Patrick?'

'Left holding the babbies, or in his case the nappies.'

'You've got a nerve,' Margaret had said and not in total admiration. 'And, Seonaid, are you not a Catholic? I'd have thought all this would be against your principles.'

'Sure, not when a life's at stake and I'm saving that oulde yoke Father O'Patrick's conscience too. He'd feel guilty at some point – or should do. Anyway, Margaret, you'd better stay at home tonight and pray for my soul in your own way,' said Seonaid, counting her out. 'Would anybody else like to come to the Showband? I've two tickets.'

The rest of the group declined and, having qualified on the grounds of being a stranger in town and not totally impoverished by buying Matron's book, I was in.

'What should I wear?'

'Tight and not tartan,' she'd advised, and now that I was back in my room, she'd come to look at a wardrobe full of stout weather-proof gear.

She was critical. 'I know we get a lot of rain, but you seem to be expecting a flood. What about this?' She picked out a dress, so small it was surprising she noticed it. 'That green'll go great with your red hair.'

I'd bought the flimsy thing in a fit of optimism and now, more realistically, was wondering why.

'It'll be fine as long as I don't breathe, and have you a shoe horn? I don't think Belfast's ready for so many curves in such a little space.' I tried to grab it to put it back but Seonaid's grip tightened. 'Ah, for God's sake! This is the Sixties, remember, it's not as if you're going to a parish meeting. You'll be super.' She rolled the 'r' in a mocking way.

'You'll be a wee while before you speak like a proper Scot, so you won't,' I jeered.

I thought I might bottle out if I looked in the mirror so, when dressed, I asked for Seonaid's opinion instead.

She looked me over carelessly. 'Grand now!' She took a tailed comb from an enormous handbag and handed it over. 'But you'll need to do a bit of back-combing right at the top.' She twiddled her finger above her head. 'With your hair that flat, nobody'll notice you.'

Tonight Miss MacCready hadn't that problem. With her hair splendidly bouffant and with a dress so shockingly pink it could have brought on a migraine, she glissaded over the foyer floor to greet us.

'Youse two planning to go out then?'

'Yes,' said Seonaid, taking my arm as if I needed special assistance. 'Jane needs to see a bit of the town and its rich heritage.'

Miss MacCready cast a glance about her then whispered, 'It wouldn't be a blind date then?'

'Good gracious no!' I said, even if the idea had some appeal.

Miss MacCready looked doubtful. 'I'm pleased to hear it. Ye see, I'd the same conversation with a wee nurse who'd just arrived here from the country. Lovely girl she was, so she was, and just like you she was going out and dressed much the same.'

90

Having made reproof as obvious as the draught swirling about my knees, she went on, 'She told me someone from an agency had fixed her up with a date.'

A night porter wheezed into sight. Coldly, the receptionist watched as he hung his jacket over a hard chair before sitting down. 'How are ye, Jo?' she asked, not bothering for a reply but returning to her saga. 'Well, off she went into the night saying, "That's me off, Miss MacCready – and I'm so excited."' With a breath intake enough to resite the pink, she held up two fingers. '*Two* days later she came back … and…'

At this rate we were going to miss all buses heading into town. Sneakily, I checked my watch but Miss MacCready didn't notice – she was on a roll. 'She didn't know where she'd been nor,' she paused for a moment, looked shiftily at Jo as if a man reading a newspaper constituted danger, then, bending low, she whispered, 'who she'd been with!'

A kirby grip fell to the floor, the bouffant threatened to topple, then straightening and cranking up the volume she continued, crying in genuine horror, 'Or how many!'

Jo shook his paper like someone reading something much more interesting whilst Miss MacCready righted herself, looked at her watch and sighed. 'Anyway, I should be off duty. Jo here will let you in when and if you come back. Now hurry or you'll miss that bus.'

'We'll be very careful,' we reassured her and tramped out into a night where the most threatening of company was an evil little wind. It pounced on us as if lonely. Clamouring for attention it whooped and whined, tugging and plucking on clothes so lacking in tartan, hypothermia seemed inevitable. It wailed in a desolate way as we caught the bus and stepped into a fag-filled fug no wind could dissipate.

Clad in a frill mostly, Seonaid seemed impervious to the cold and sat glued to the window of our bus as it racketed down the Falls Road past its tenement houses, a news vender provocatively bawling *'Protestant Cooorrier,* sixpence only!' small shops fluttering orange and green flags, pawn brokers and big churches. Finally, we arrived at the warmer flirty girl that was Belfast's city centre.

There were glamorous clothes in brightly-lit shop windows. They promised sophistication likely to feature in the nearby hotels and restaurants and where a student midwife's monthly pay could have gone on the first course. The more tangible prospect of fish 'n' chips was on offer along busy streets where music spilt out from crowded bars.

'Do you not have singing pubs then?' asked Seonaid, fingers sliding over a pokeful of grease. We were standing in a queue of depressingly pretty girls all apparently heading for Seonaid's promised evening of local culture.

'No. Drinking in Scotland is considered a serious affair demanding single-minded attention, and if folk want to hear music they go home and listen to their trannies or records.'

'They don't sound like party people. Even if I haven't a player at least I have a record. Herb Alpert. He's great for parties.' Seonaid emptied the bag into her mouth, tidying its corner with a delicate finger. 'Anytime I get invited anywhere, I take my record with me so I get to hear it.'

'Maybe you could get another, or be radical – go for a complete change and buy one from them, start a collection.' I nodded at a Bedford bus parked nearby with the Showband's name palsy-hand painted on its side and from which the band was now descending.

'Sure, the one I've got's plenty and it's boring carrying too much stuff.' She folded the bag tidily then popped it in my pocket. 'Look, we're moving.'

The queue streamed into a barn of a place where a Daisy look-alike exchanged our coats for a ticket before adding them to the pile on her desk.

'And there'll be no smoking,' she adjured,

which was surprising considering that once into the hall proper it was so smoke-filled we could just make out the band on a platform at the far end.

'They'll be the warm-ups, come on!'

I followed Seonaid as she pushed her way to the front to see a group in such bright gear they looked like a row of Wurlitzers. Despite the lead singer, cough mixture bottle in hand, pouring his heart into a song of betrayal in Belfast, the audience was unimpressed and felt particularly free to say so.

'Can ye not think of another tune, we're sick of hearing that oulde yoke,' someone shouted whilst a penny landed on the stage.

Without missing a beat the guitarist picked it up and flung it back. 'It's a bad penny!' he shouted, which was just enough to trigger a steady metal downpour and give a whole new meaning to the term 'warming up'.

'So come all you jolly young fellows,' continued the singer, now unaccompanied on account of his team fully occupied returning fire, 'a warning take by me.'

'You've missed out a verse,' shouted someone who must have thought it safe to shout from the back.

An argument broke out, followed by a scuffle, and soon the place was heaving with people firing pennies and shoving to get to the front. Valiantly the singer continued, de-

94

termined to finish his set before his Friar's Balsam ran out.

The band started to pocket the money and make way for the Showband, whilst running out of steam and ammunition, the audience started to settle down and chat as if this was an evening of genteel social interaction. Close by I glimpsed, deep in conversation with a leggy brunette, one of our medical students. In the conservative gear of a bank manager he looked like he was promoting the joy of saving to a spendthrift customer.

'I see your man's here.' Seonaid had spotted his friend, sartorially clad in a flowery pink shirt and purple hipsters. His white patent leather belt looked like a bandage restraining a Guinness gut.

'He's not my man,' I said. 'And by the look of things the other one's not hers either.' The brunette had stomped off, presumably taking her overdraft with her whilst the bank manager wandered off, loosening his tie, as if suddenly unemployed.

The Showband took the stage with the confidence of men who knew a thing or two about music and, in their spiv padded-shouldered suits, self defence. A quick nod amongst themselves, a trumpeted intro, then in perfect unison they blasted forth. Like a response to an activating switch, the hall became a hot, sweaty, throbbing vortex of flying heels and jiving moves.

'Are ye dancin?' The floor bounced, the music swung and Seonaid, with her asking partner, began to move at such gyroscopic speed their clothes blurred into a white to match his belt.

On account of my limited stride I had to settle for a stately saloon drive round the floor with a red-faced farmer up for a night in the city who found the noise and smoke so overwhelming he suggested a turn outside. Having learnt that Irish talk could mean different things, I declined.

'Suit yourself,' he shrugged, meaning 'your loss', and minutes later I saw him dancing with someone less restricted. Hours later and using a red lightly grease-garnished hanky to mop his brow, he was still apparently coping without farm-fresh air and staying for the last chord.

'We're getting a lift home from Raymond and Oliver,' said Seonaid, throwing on her coat. 'They're going our way.'

'You mean the likely lads?'

'Uh-huh. They've got a van. It's red, Raymond says it's his, we can't miss it and we should meet outside.'

Still miffed by the farmer I hoped he noticed us climbing aboard a tomato on wheels. It was fun if you relished a contortionist challenge of sitting in the back on the floor and didn't mind your dress and knees hiked up to your neck. I was sitting on something hard. It was another ancient pelvis. The Belfast Midwifery School must be buying them in bulk.

'I see you've brought the family heirloom,' I said to Oliver, who was already installed in the front passenger seat.

'Mind how you go with that – we need it for Prof. McQuaid's lecture. If we don't get the dreaded Mechanism lecture, we're out.'

As he sat grim-faced, I could have suggested there were alternative careers, even if graduation from a charm school might prove difficult, but I didn't fancy walking home, and Raymond with a carefree laugh was already throwing himself into the driver's seat.

'Welcome aboard, girls! I see you've met Oliver. You'll have to forgive me friend. He's got a broken heart. His girlfriend's just gone and ditched him, so she has.'

'I'll get over it but not being thrown out of medicine so mind what you do with that pelvis.' Oliver was sour.

'Here! You look after it then. We've got our own.' Seonaid thrust it at him. 'Listen.' She snapped elastic of a personal nature. 'That's me own pelvic girdle and at least ours are always with us.'

We collapsed in girlish mirth whilst Oliver emanated disapproval and Raymond shouting, 'Gas!' shot through red traffic lights managing to include a kerb or two.

I asked if Oliver's relationship had been

long-term. Bent on gloom, he nodded. 'Four years.'

'Crivvens! You must've been courting in short trousers.'

Raymond slapped the steering wheel in amusement. 'It's the way you say it! Courrt-in' in shorrrt trrousers!' He managed to beat another set of lights before the exhaust pipe rattled and fell off.

Unconcerned, he said, 'Ach, sure, at least they'll hear us coming,' and putting his foot down hard, hit the Falls Road fast.

In the watches of the night it looked even less inviting, with the churches in darkness and the smaller buildings cowering under them as if they'd been bullied into submission. We raced past small, shuttered shops, barred businesses and a closed cinema. It might have been a perfect setting for a horror movie but at least there was nobody around to complain about noise until we reached Bostock House and Jo came out to investigate.

'Would ye be stopping that racket now,' he said, peering into the car. 'If the MacCready was here she'd have had you arrested.'

9

HARD LABOUR

Bar a day in the week under Miss Harvey's governessy care, we were now getting experience in the hospital proper. I was in the Labour Suite and constantly worried about who was coming through those swing doors. Every patient admitted would need reassurance, an assessment, then constant vigilant care. Since everybody's needs were different, the work was challenging.

It was a relief to get off duty and join Seonaid. We went to see Marie, whose agonies over work with the tinies in the Special Care Nursery started to make the labour ward feel like a course in relaxation.

'It's a terrible responsibility, so it is,' sighed Marie, 'and desperate hard to imagine any of them surviving. All those little lives hanging by a thread.' She looked at her hands, spread them and held them up. 'Some of them are no bigger than these and I can't stop wondering what's going to happen to them if and when they get home. They're just so helpless.'

Seonaid stopped bouncing on the bed for

a moment. 'Well, here's something to cheer ye up. I've good news about Mrs Murphy. She's in my post-natal ward and recovering faster from her Caesarean than finding her old fella's kindly allowed her to have a sterilisation. Now would that not warm your little oulde heart?' She slid off the bed and did a graceful pirouette.

It didn't impress Marie. 'I suppose so, but what about the babby?' She sighed and rubbed her brow. 'Everybody's talked about that mammy and daddy but d'you notice nobody's ever mentioned the wee dote? It's as if he's just an item.' If it had been anybody else but Marie she'd have sounded angry. 'Sure an' he must have had an awful shock arriving in the world so quickly.'

'Better than squashed through a tunnel sideways.' Seonaid was dismissive. 'And he's grand. Lovely wee fella. Doin' well. Thriving.'

'Thanks be to–' Marie's look dared me to interrupt '–God!'

I said nothing so she rushed on. 'Some of my poor wee lambs are so frail they might die without even being christened.' She twisted her hands in anguish and bit her lip.

'I'm sure God won't mind.' I meant it kindly. 'I expect he's got a nice selection of names for them to choose from.'

Marie allowed herself a crafty smile. 'Ah, but he won't have to bother. I give them a

100

wee christening when nobody's looking.'

'Well I hope you whisper it,' said Seonaid, suddenly looked serious. 'Different faiths mightn't like you putting yours in over theirs. Anyway, what names do you give them?'

'That's easy! Marie or Mario. Anyway, God'll change them if need be – and,' Marie was triumphant, 'I just say it inside my head when I'm taking a drop of water from the incubator's cooling system to make a wee cross on their foreheads. They don't seem to mind and at least if anything does happen to them God'll know they've already been blessed.' The thought seemed to cheer her up.

The next day on my way past the nursery I wondered what names were swirling about those incubator occupants Marie was so zealously christening. At least Mary-Jo was already named, and actually giving Marie a rare moment of optimism.

'She's thriving, out of her incubator, and making such progress she'll soon be running the Nursery.' Marie gave a fond chuckle. 'Then her mammy's getting confident handling her, and even her daddy's been in. Handling her like a professional and dying to get her home. It shouldn't be long now.'

However, I couldn't linger. Sister Flynn's demanding punctuality ruled, so I hurried to the Labour Suite from which this morning not even the unborn would be exempt.

'Come on now, Nurse Macpherson, we've a whole morning of overdue babies to induce and you're late.' She had the slight figure of an athlete with a running step that made you feel breathless just watching. Now she was hurtling a loaded trolley towards me at such breakneck speed I thought she mightn't brake in time.

'Here. This soap needs diluting.' She took a jar from the trolley and thrust it at me. 'The whole hospital's crying for it. Hurry on now!' Sounding like a late milk float, the trolley with its driver flashed past.

Given that I was not yet allowed near a patient other than for chasing autographs to prove I'd witnessed deliveries, making an elixir of enema soap must be a sign of promotion. I went to the cubbyhole of a kitchen where the sink was stacked full of dirty dishes and the cooker looked like a discarded chip supper.

I knew that when administered via a rectal tube, enema soap caused a dramatic rush to the toilet, but I didn't know much about its other properties. On a voyage of discovery, I threw a handful of the thick green soapy glue into a big pan of boiling water and stirred.

'I'm off to antenatal to get our first patient, so hurry up. We haven't all day and you're always so slow.' Sister Flynn was charging out of the Labour Suite. Her voice floated back, taking the air of urgency with it. I wondered what she did to relax – probably whizz through a book of timetables.

Staff Midwife McQuarry came to investigate. She brightened up the place with her Doris Day looks and ability to burst into song to celebrate everyday things. Today she was especially cheerful. 'Happy days are here again,' she sang, throwing a packet of sanitary towels in the air and catching it with the poise of a ball game expert. 'So what's cooking?'

The mixture had come to a nice rolling boil with green bubbles attractively frothing the surface then spattering over onto the cooker and explaining its greasy marks.

'Welcome to the soap kitchen. Want a taste?' I offered her a spoonful.

'Ach, but you're a card,' she said, 'but no thanks. It's strong and black stuff I'm after and it's not Guinness before you say it. Now where's that coffee?'

'Try behind the bread bin,' I suggested, wondering who'd eat anything from such a rusting bucket and relieved when she looked in, found nothing and saved herself from food poisoning.

'The boys have been here.' She sounded exasperated. 'You'd think they'd leave something for the workers. I suppose I'll just have to settle for plain coffee on its own.' She spooned in enough to guarantee a caffeine overdose then made the hot water pour from a height to waterfall splash into her mug.

'Makes all the difference,' she said, smacking her lips. 'Now you be sure to label that brew, we wouldn't want it going in the wrong orifice.'

'For such a lovely girl, Lisa, you can be quite common.' Dr Welch had strolled in, sitting down on the only chair and looking around as if expecting a waitress. 'Is there another cup?'

Lisa pulled on a blonde curl, which corkscrewed right back as she nodded at the sink. 'You'll have to wash one first. Jane here'll give you something to wash one with, and before you ask, there's no biscuits either.' The empty bin now seemed to please her.

'Mind your pinny.' I splashed in a ladlefull of bubbles. 'And be sure and rinse that out unless you've been swearing lately and need your mouth cleaned out. Look,' I handed him a dishtowel. 'You'll need that for drying.'

'I think I'll take my custom elsewhere.' He got up then, reaching the door, asked casually if Lisa was going to the Medic's Ball.

'Course I am,' she said. 'Jimmy asked me.'

'Ah, the luck of O'Reilly.' He sounded disappointed and drifted off.

I'd stopped stirring and now peered into

the depths of the pan.

'One of our crowd's taken an awful shine to that bloke,' I said, slightly alarmed at the toffee-like lump sticking to the bottom. 'He could ask her.'

'She'd be welcome.' Lisa drained the last of her coffee and gave an exasperated sigh. 'He's so slow he could do with a rocket up his arse.' She sniffed and looked puzzled. 'And what would you say's that smell?'

I was glad she wasn't watching as I quickly poured the unstuck mixture into a jug, moved into bottling mode and slid a badly burnt pan out of sight.

Sister Flynn would be furious. Her precious pot was going to need some serious scrubbing and would have to remain hidden until I could take it with me off duty. The prospect of an evening dealing with a burnt pan was an item only likely to appeal to Marie as an addition to her disaster collection.

Lisa pointed to a freshly-filled bottle. 'I'm just glad I don't need any of that. It doesn't usually have that smell, but come on now. How many more witnessed deliveries do you need before you get your own freckled hand on a baby's head?'

'Bagged the last one yesterday.' I was quietly triumphant, especially as neither Cynthia nor Margaret, stuck in the ante-natal clinic, were near this stage.

On the positive side however, Margaret's makeup expertise was improving with her lipstick now aiming in the right direction. She was even developing listening skills, not something much required in her previous life in theatre.

Having been handed a huge bottle of urine with a week's worth in it, Cynthia was also learning, but by a hard way. 'They don't seem to understand. I'm only needing a few drops to test their urine,' she said in frustration.

Margaret couldn't let that pass. 'Well, that's the Irish for you, generous to a fault. I expect that wouldn't be a problem in your London Hospital.'

'Ah! You see – that's why I'm here,' Cynthia was all sweetness and light, 'to help the people with their problems.'

I was dying to lord a first delivery over them and told Lisa so.

'Right! I'll have a word with Flynnie. Look she's back with that patient – can't you hear her marching her through? Probably telling her the walk'll do her good.' Lisa chuckled and, draining the last of her coffee, chucked the mug into the sink. 'Come on. This'd be a good chance to get you started.'

Which is probably what must have been said to Denise who was our patient and whose distended fingers and puffy face made her look like a blown-up version of the original.

After a discussion that seemed to involve Sister Flynn shaking her head like a metronome against Lisa's ultimately successful counterbalance, the news was broken to Denise waiting in the corridor, her elfin if swollen beauty turning it into a palace of sorts.

'Would you mind Nurse Macpherson helping you with your labour? She's really keen and very competent.' Lisa's confidence was breathtaking.

'I've met her already,' said Denise in a damning sort of way.

'That's grand then! Come on now, let's get you into bed. I see your locker's come with you too. Good! It'll save us transferring all your stuff.' Lisa led the prisoner into her cell and helped her climb aboard, then laid out on an overbed table enough charts and paperwork to start a typing pool riot.

Patting them in an affectionate sort of way, she explained, 'These are so we can record the baby's heart, your heart, contractions and strength, waterworks, blood pressure, and your drip monitor if it's fitted. Nurse Macpherson's going to do that and keep you company as well.' Lisa made it all sound like the start of a great party.

Sister Flynn came in and being a busy, important person she disregarded Denise's look of doubt and anxiety and wagged a finger. She had the single-minded look of a blackbird pulling on a worm. 'I'm sure Nurse Macpherson's going to be fine. She's been shown how to do these readings often enough, and if an induction's on the cards it might all take a little time so she'll get plenty practice.' Then, as if unaware she might be compounding the problem, she added, 'Of course, we wouldn't have to do it if your blood pressure was stable.' She sighed and tapped her watch. 'You'll have to have an enema first. Ah, but time's the divil!' The hint that it was all Denise's fault hung loud.

'But this is my first,' Denise protested.

'Mine too, Denise,' I could have said if I didn't have to clamp my mouth over chattering teeth. Moving from spectator to participant was suddenly a scary prospect and Denise's nervousness didn't help.

Compared to her farm home, the labour ward with its beige walls, grey flooring and clinical furnishing must have had all the appeal of a grim institution. She looked about her fearfully. Her swollen fingers, like sickly starfish, clutched her dressing gown. She wasn't wearing the sparkler but maybe this wasn't the time to ask about it. Hopefully it was safe in the hospital security vaults.

I tried for a bright tone. 'Does your husband know you'll be having the baby soon?'

'Yes. He says he wants to be with me.'

Denise's voice trailed off uncertainly whilst Sister Flynn reacted as if at a starter's gun, her feet already in the running position, her brow in a disapproving furrow. 'Well, let's get going – no time to be standing about gassing or waiting for husbands.' She said it with such disparagement Denise must have got the message that her husband had already served his purpose. 'But you're in good hands. There's the medical team here as well as Nurse Macpherson, and there'll be Mr Allan.'

Denise brightened and smoothed her hair. 'Is he a doctor then?'

Sister Flynn moved into selling mode. 'No. He's a medical student. He's here for some labour ward experience and is already proving he's very good.'

And a misery guts, I thought as Oliver appeared, looking earnest with a notebook in hand and a stethoscope necklace lending suitable gravitas. He walked round the bed with the anxious step of a man used to missing buses.

'Hello, Denise. I hope you don't mind but I'll be taking your history whilst she,' he nodded at me, 'will be recording your progress and doing any needful nursing chores.'

At least I was going to be on the right side of the enema funnel, I might have said. Instead I went for just the right amount of sugar. 'That's right – as well as attending to some delicate procedures, so why don't you go and sharpen your little pencil whilst we girls get on with the real work.'

His mouth opened but whether in surprise or with a stunning reply we will never know because the doors flew open admitting a patient at the height of labour.

'Oh, look! Excuse me, Denise, but there's a good chance I'll get my last witness now,' he almost looked enthusiastic, 'and then I'll get back to you and then – who knows – I might even get to deliver you.' He cantered off after the cavalcade heading for the labour ward, a man determined to catch this particular bus.

'I wish I wasn't here,' said Denise, showing poor faith but heaving herself out of bed and following me to a soapy future in a room within sprinting distance of a toilet.

10

HANDS-ON CARE

More drastic measures were needed to get the baby on the move. Denise's baby had apparently reasoned that the unpleasant nature of an enema administered to its mother was a good reason for staying put.

After a little discussion with Dr O'Reilly and a lot of reassurance from Lisa, she was wheeled into a delivery room.

'Don't go away,' said Denise, holding onto my hand. Then she submitted herself to the internal and secure bag of water, which had been the baby's home for so long, being popped. I was glad she didn't see the instrument used by Dr O'Reilly. It frighteningly resembled a crotchet hook.

A strong contraction and irritated kick shifting the shape of Denise's abdomen meant the baby had got the message and was already beginning to flit.

Dr O'Reilly said, 'That's good. We've now ruptured your membranes and your internal examination shows that your labour has started.' He pulled off his gloves and slung them along with the recently used instrument into a kidney dish. 'Get rid of these will you?'

Sister Flynn took them with a sigh, giving a hard look at Denise who, clinging onto my hand, had no intention of letting go.

'I've to do everything around here,' she said and threw them into a sink with such a clatter the sound seemed to bounce on the bleak walls then hang overhead like an angry reproach. Ignoring the noise, Dr O'Reilly patted Denise's leg as if to soothe. 'We'll also put up a drip – see if we can hurry things along.'

Not being in control of much else, Denise widened her eyes and fluttered her eyelashes. 'You're very gentle, Doctor. It's good to know I'm in your hands.'

'That's the girl, but let's see what you can do now.' He spoke in a preoccupied way, watching Dr Welch who had come in and was idly chatting to Lisa.

'Excuse me, I've a few more patients to attend to, but Dr Welch over there seems underemployed so I'll get him to do the rest.'

'Dr Welch's been an absolute saint,' began Denise but Dr O'Reilly had gone and the houseman was coming towards her, looking as if he'd had a row.

Since Sister Flynn had probably tidied William away in a husband-containing cupboard, there was still no sign of him, and in the absence of any other comforter and just in case Dr Welch's wonderful touch had gone, Denise continued the hand grip. Only once she was back in her own bed and realised I might have to climb in with her did she let go.

'You'll need to keep a close watch on the readings,' Lisa had warned, wrinkling her brow and looking unusually anxious. 'Sister Flynn thinks this is quite a difficult case and you haven't enough experience, but I've told her you're more capable than you look, so keep a close eye on her blood pressure and that foetal heart. Any drastic change and you'll need to tell us, but we're really busy at the moment so don't press the panic button unless you're sure you need to.' She rubbed her forehead whilst in the distance an ambulance siren sounded. 'Ach! That's maybe for us. The place's goin' daft alright.' She bustled off.

Denise, perkier now, fluffed up her hair and settled back on her pillows. '"Mad house" she says, but this is better than that oulde labour theatre place, though you'd hardly call here home sweet home. Is it any wonder my blood pressure's up?'

She tapped her hand over her mouth. 'But at least I've stopped being sick.'

She looked so relieved I was glad she hadn't read the chapter on eclampsia that had been dealt with in such gory detail in the textbooks it was enough to ratchet up any law-abiding heartbeat.

This wasn't the time to be competitive but the worry of Denise was already giving me palpitations. Not for the first time in a career on which I was so determined, I wondered why on earth I was pursuing it. It was bad enough having responsibility for one, never mind two, even if the second had sentenced its mother to a nine-month puke. Denise's rocketing blood pressure could lead to a 'bad news all round' eclamptic fit whilst still to come was the actual birth!

My stroke would just have to wait.

'Every baby is an individual,' Miss Harvey had intoned, 'and so nobody can actually say for sure how quickly they will arrive. Sometimes,' she had given a little chortle, 'the little rascals can surprise even the most professional of midwives, so you need to keep a lookout all the time.'

Unsure how to define 'lookout' other than peeking under the sheets whilst listening for unusual sounds, I was convinced that, with each contraction, this little rascal of a baby would arrive. Presumably one born in a bed would get me black marks. If I didn't read the signs accurately and Denise didn't get transferred to the labour ward in time it would figure badly in my record book as well as putting Margaret and Cynthia's superiority at an all-time high. I put my hand on Denise's abdomen and felt its hard contraction.

Oh Lord! Was this it?

Denise moved restlessly.

'You alright?' I asked, finger hovering over the panic button.

She raised an eyebrow. 'Never better, and would ye calm down? You're making me nervous, so ye are.' She reached towards her locker, pushing aside the sickness bowl. 'I don't think I'm needing that. Now where's me *Ulster Farmer's* magazine?' She sounded a different girl – presumably her sickness had joined the baby in moving out.

'Denise! You're full of surprises. I thought *Ulster Fashion Tips* would be more your line.'

'Ye thought wrong then, didn't you,' said Denise, waving the magazine. 'Us farmers need to keep up with what's going on. Now put away that eau de cologne you keeping drowning me with and see if there's any messages from that baby.'

Pleased with her humour, I put the stethoscope in place, closed my eyes and listened. My heartbeat was so loud I wondered why my textbooks hadn't offered any handy tips on screening out such competition.

'Hello! I'm back. I've just had my last witness,' announced Oliver from the doorway. Now, apparently qualified as a self-appointed advisor, he strolled in, pursing his lips to convey serious intent whilst folding his arms and looking over the charts as if they were ledgers.

'Hello, Denise,' he said, favouring her with a smile that made him look like a friendly ferret. 'Things coming along fine are they? Thought I'd just see how you're both faring.'

I presumed he meant the baby but he was raising his eyebrows and pointing to a graph that, before I'd gone deaf, had recorded a baby's very fast heartbeat. It was about to go off scale. This baby must be doing circuit training, but surely it was time to get it off the treadmill. Any more of this and I'd not only be getting more graph paper, I'd be ringing that bell.

'Uh-huh. You'll need to watch this,' he breathed.

'What're you whispering about?' asked Denise, suddenly looking anxious enough to tear herself from the fascinations of pig breeding. 'Is everything all right there?'

'Absolutely fine. If Mr Allan would just shush, I'd get a good listen. See what's the news.'

As the baby clocked another round, I took another reading and breathed easier. This was better. It must be taking a rest – even Denise's blood pressure was back on track. I must read that article on pigs, I thought, it might relax me too.

Oliver had fetched a chair and sat down, saying in a smug way, 'Thanks for waiting. I can't wait to start on my deliveries, and if you'd like me to do yours, Denise, I'm sure Nurse Macpherson here'll get plenty opportunity for others.' He sat back, crossed his arms and legs and admired shoes so highly polished they competed with Miss Harvey's.

Even though things were beginning to settle down, Denise's labour seemed so fraught with danger that if Oliver was determined to get this delivery he could have it. Then I could cancel my stroke, deal with the burnt pan and at least get one problem off the premises.

'Tell you what, *Mr* Allan.' I shoved Denise's paperwork into a bundle and thrust it at him. 'Why don't you take these readings as well? Then you'll be finely placed to ensure she has a perfect delivery.'

Denise's fairly benign state transformed into Sisters Unite as she put her paper down and squawked, 'An' what about me? I notice you're not even asking me. You're not thinking of leaving me with him now! I want you here.' An imperious, if swollen, finger waggled. 'Just hearing you speak makes me laugh – you've such a quair oulde way of talking. A traitorous tear rolled down that alabaster cheek whilst she moved into weenie voice. 'The boys are alright but a girl needs another she can talk to

Maybe having a baby on the move gets a mother's brain back. Denise was certainly picking up steam. The finger moved to Oliver. 'I've been sick all my pregnancy and now I'm sick of being asked the same thing all the time. You said you'd be taking my history. Well, that's history.' She shook her head and rolled her eyes.

Oh Lord! These were classic eclamptic symptoms. Surely she wasn't having a fit! Had I left things too long. Time froze, but just as I reached for the bell she added, 'I don't think you listen anyway and,' her pout was one of her finest, her timing immaculate, 'you're just a student.'

Oliver, looking abashed, shot up and held up both hands. 'Of course, Denise, whatever you say. I'm sorry. I didn't mean to upset you. I'm not here to do that and of course I'll not ask any questions.' He brushed back his hair, patting it down at the back as if scared it might take off. 'Look! It's probably best that I just go.' He headed for the door, his brow furrowed anxiously. 'Look, that's me away now, OK?'

'That's another feckin' question,' she replied, picking at an imaginary thread off the bedclothes then lifting her paper.

'I'll be around if you need me, Janet,' Oliver mouthed and walked off in a bus-losing sort of way.

Denise slid down in her bed, looking pleased. 'Now you can tell me how things are really doin'? That fella made me nervous, so he did, and he was looking so worried, it was making me even worse.'

I pinned on a smile, 'Everything's fine but you're like a wee clucking hen and I'll be thinking you're sitting on a China egg if we don't see that chick of yours soon.' I hoped to sound encouraging.

A glimmer of humour showed in Denise's pale face. 'Well, it's a pity it's not one. I like hens.'

'Better than babies?'

She smoothed the sheet and gave it close attention. 'Probably. I haven't had any experience of them. We haven't been married that long. I'm only just getting used to a change of name and now my shape's so different.' She spread her fingers, nodding at them. 'Even they don't look as if they belong.'

'I wouldn't have put you as a hen wife,' I mused, 'but you sure are clocking up the contractions. Just feel that.' I put her hand on her bump, but she didn't seem impressed.

'Does that all the time.'

Diligently I recorded *strong* 1–3, meaning *any minute now*. Before I took her pulse, I discreetly checked mine, ashamed when I found it beat hers.

But an unaware Denise was warming to her hen theme. 'Now Rhode Island Reds, they're great layers. The first batch were coming on great – eggs everywhere – lovely colour of yolks, and a nice bit of pin money for me too so I was planning more when this came along.' She pointed to her bump, her shoulders drooped and she sounded defeated.

'Next thing you'll be telling me you're a whizz on the tractor.'

Denise sat up, throwing back her hair as if it were blowing in the wind and she were a rally driver. 'I really like the driving, especially now that we've got a new one. I chose the colour but it's William's pride and joy. He says he doesn't really like me on it.

Says I go too fast, but I just tell him the quicker the better.' Her eyes sparkled and she had such colour in her cheeks I just hoped her blood pressure hadn't noticed.

I tried for a big sister approach. 'Tell that to that baby of yours and, for what it's worth, Denise, it sounds to me that you're coping pretty well already. Not many people can say they've become a tractor man, hen wife, farmer, wife as well as an about-to-be mother. And what about William then? Is he excited about becoming a father?'

'Oh sure – but then he didn't have to carry it.'

'No, but he can after it's born.'

Denise looked thoughtful. 'I never really thought about that.' She giggled, putting her hand in front of her mouth as if to stifle such an unnatural sound. 'So when it comes to pushing he'll get his chance with the pram.'

'Too much laughter in here!' Sister Flynn whirled in.

I imagined that if people had clockwork for brains Sister Flynn's would run like a trade union clock, its wheels whirring away in well-oiled precision. You could almost hear them ticking as she checked the progress charts on which I had so toiled.

'Hmm.' With nursing skill and a plumber's confidence, she tweaked the valve of Denise's labour-inducing intravenous drip to ramp up her contractions.

'Ow!' squeaked Denise.

'Ah! That's better. Let's be getting a move on. That baby's a dozy wee thing.' She bumped her hand over Denise's belly. 'Uh-huh! Contractions getting stronger. Good good.' Sucking her teeth over the record sheets, she dashed out again.

'That woman gives me a sore head,' Denise said, putting a hand to her forehead, 'as well as makes me dizzy.' She clutched her stomach and gave a little moan. 'I think I need a bedpan.'

I looked at her closely. 'You're not feeling like pushing?'

'No! But hurry.'

'Trust me. I've helped many a princess onto her silver throne but don't you be having that baby whilst I'm away getting it. I'll only be a minute.'

'Sure, having babies takes a little longer than that, they tell me,' she said, squirming.

'Goodness – did I hear light-hearted talk? That's great. So how's things doing?' Lisa asked, joining Oliver who, in the absence of anything better to do, had been loitering at the sluice door in time to watch my return, bedpan in hand. 'Bet you're nervous, first delivery and all that, though you seem to be getting on grand.' She looked at Oliver. 'I thought you were staying to help?'

Oliver waved a careless hand. 'Thought I'd give Denise a bit of space – she's been seen by so many, I thought it best.' He shrugged and looked at his watch. 'So maybe this is a chance for me to nip off and have a coffee before the action starts and maybe a wee word of advice, Janet.' He cleared his throat, whilst moving into *how to manage finances, You Little Person,* mode. 'I'd look more in control. That poor girl's anxious enough without you looking as if you're having her every pain. Every time you put on the sphygmomanometer to take her pressure and pump up the cuff, she goes green.'

'Same colour as this.' My laugh was hollow as well as disbelieving whilst I pointed to the testing paper fresh from testing the bedpan's water content.

'What a cheek you've got!'

I could have gone to town on him but I needed to get back to my patient.

'Look!' I snapped. 'This shows there's enough protein in her urine to feed Africa. Somebody's got to look out for her kidneys. With all the strain they're under it shows they're not managing to work properly. No wonder I'm worried, but as for being cool and calm, I think *my* patient trusts me.'

'Of course. Whatever you say.'

'Well then, I think I'd say you've a better future in anaesthetics,' I snapped before going back to Denise who seemed mightily relieved to see me.

Her face was pink and she said in a strangled voice, 'I'm beginning to feel like pushing.'

'Right!' I said, 'So am I,' and pressed the emergency button.

11

AND IT'S A FIRST!

Whilst Denise's pregnancy had been a lousy nine months, her labour was at least, for a first-time baby and perhaps due to all that tractor drill, a relatively short affair.

'First stage complete.' Sister Flynn was as pleased as if she were a stationmaster with all trains running on time. 'With a bit of luck, the second stage shouldn't take long either. Go and scrub up, Nurse Macpherson. I think I'll conduct this delivery.'

'And I've found Denise's husband! To be sure he was thinking you'd forgotten about him.' Lisa sounded triumphant. 'Stuck in the waiting room – he'll be through in a minute.'

Her curls made a fluffy halo but Sister Flynn, unimpressed by random cherubs, merely said, 'On his own head be it. We can't be having him holding up the works.'

Not like me, I thought, scrubbing my hands and trying to feed them into rubber gloves, so large two fingers got trapped together. To my horror they stuck, as if welded together.

Unaware of my frantic fumbling, Lisa locked me into an enormous sterile gown with such insulating quality that had it not been for the cold sweat trickling down my spine, I could have dissolved.

'Come on, Jane, let's go. You don't want to miss this one, do you?'

'Um, Lisa…'

But she'd gone, leaving me no other option than to tuck the unoccupied rubber finger into my palm.

'You're ready to go, and it'll be great, just wait and see.' Lisa reappeared and now was at my shoulder. She propelled me forward. 'Now I'll need to get that husband ready before Flynnie makes up an excuse to keep him out. She's really the limit. But I'm thinking I've won this round, and at the end of it all maybe one husband might just not think having a baby's a piece of cake.' The curls bounced as she added that she'd put Oliver in charge of taking Denise's blood pressure. 'Told him he needed the practice.' Chuckling, she sped off, Tinker Bell on a mission.

'Come on, come on!' came Flynn's scolding voice. 'If you don't come now, you're going to miss it.'

There was every chance that was what I might just do. Being one finger down and trussed up like a mobile greenhouse I approached the delivery table. At least Denise wasn't complaining that Oliver had been co-opted, even if his fountain pen was blotching ink all over the previously pristine charts. All other attention was being trained on the baby's exit strategy, where a brief sighting had encouraged a small crowd into a spectator sport.

Oliver's girlfriend was there too – she must have been a medical student clocking up her witnessing stats. Conscientiously, Oliver concentrated on his readings, looking sufficiently pale and heroic enough to be a main player. I hoped she was impressed.

'There it is. We can see it but we need to see more, so come on now, you can do it this time. Push!' Sister Flynn was a decibel short of shouting whilst Denise groaned, cursed and writhed.

'You're not pushing properly. Come on! You can do better than this.'

'Oh shut up and do it yourself. So help me, William can have the next one. Where is he?' Denise shook her head as if trying to free herself from a barbed wire pillow. 'I'm being split in half. Somebody do something please!' The cry was heart rending. She grabbed the

Entonox and took a deep draught before Sister Flynn snatched it away, saying, 'That's making you woozy. Now, use your energy to *push!*' She really should enrol for a charm school. Maybe she and Oliver could cut a deal and get it half price.

'Nurse! Get your hand ready to cover that baby's head. Smartly now.'

This was probably the time for the discovery of digital deficiency but the miraculous new appearance of a gowned and masked individual diverted all attention elsewhere.

Sister Flynn hissed, 'No! Not you! Get to the top of the table.'

Had it not been for the twitching eyes and sweating forehead the figure making a fast relocation could have been just another doctor.

'William! I thought you'd never get here.' Denise's welcome was marginally better though he was soon told off for smoothing her brow, patting her head, telling her to push and being responsible for her being stretched on this bed of misery. Lisa fetched him a seat, though he was so visibly trembling he looked as if he might fall off.

'Yez are all telling me to push but I can't any longer. Yez'll have to do something to help. I can't do all the work.' Denise's voice was beginning to get faint, her hair was wet with sweat and lay in ropey coils over her shoulders, her hands flailed the air and she was so pale she'd have made a corpse look healthy.

Hang in there, Denise, I thought, you've come so far and in so many ways and taken me with you.

We seemed to have reached stalemate but at least I'd my floating rubber finger firmly tucked out of sight. Though it wasn't likely to be hidden much longer it was rapidly becoming the least of my worries. The small bit of head showing was slippery and time was running out. Denise was plainly exhausted. Dr O'Reilly was beginning to look round, wondering where the forceps pack was. There was mounting tension under the spotlight, with the baby apparently stuck and the foetal heart registering distress.

Around a circle of clinical light, an ominous silence descended whilst William looked as if he might faint and Denise as if she already had. Oliver started to chew his pen then recorded a trajectory so blotched it looked like an exclamation mark. His girl-friend, coming out in sympathy, bit her lip.

Time was of the essence. I thought about Denise and how really tough she was, but she was getting too tired to continue and that baby needed out *now*.

'Right! That's it.' Eyes trained on the spot-light, Dr O'Reilly moved to take over.

This was my last chance. I stood my

ground, squared my shoulders and took a deep breath. 'Hey, Denise, girl. Come on. It's full throttle time. Go!'

Sister Flynn looked up, startled. Maybe she'd noticed the two fingers and read a different message.

'I'm conducting this labour and I'm in charge,' she whispered, the groove between her eyebrows deepening, 'and just you let Dr O'Reilly in now! I've never seen the like.' She narrowed her eyes but still I didn't, couldn't, wouldn't budge. She upped her tone. 'I'm ordering you to shift. Move. Right away! D'ye hear?'

Outside, Belfast might be roaring and grumbling and inside there was about to be a war but I didn't care. I'd gone deaf, dazzled and delighted because a head had made its debut.

I continued, 'You've done it! Wonderful! Now! Idling time, foot off and think of...' Now what would appeal to the farmer in this wife. My mind raced, then, 'Chickens! Chook chook, Denise! That's it! Great! Now clocking time nearly over, just another wee burst for the shoulders.'

I spread the fingers of my left hand. At least, and even though it felt like a flipper, I'd got this one properly gloved. I hooked it under an emerging arm then, with both hands, helped out the little baby.

'It's a boy!'

As if on cue, sunshine glanced in the window, making the room less clinical. Denise's yell was enough to drown out the baby's but by the time the cord was cut and he was lifted, handed over and checked that he'd more fingers than the deliverer, he'd begun to successfully register. Unfortunately, so had Sister Flynn.

'I've just noticed your fingers,' she croaked. 'Tell me I'm seeing things, or have we a lunatic at large?'

'They're very big gloves.' I tried for the confident manner of a coper. 'It wasn't a problem.'

She shook her head as if ridding it of flies. 'It'll be card tricks next. You and I'll need to have a talk after all this, but in the meantime,' she turned her attention to Denise who was tracing a bawling infant's cheek and looking at him with a dazed expression, 'isn't that a grand wee son you have there?'

Denise promptly handed him to William as if she were a stolen goods fence.

'Don't drop that child!' snapped Sister Flynn, getting back into her stride and making William start. He held the baby more firmly but already the sister was looking for Lisa. 'Staff!' Doing wonders for paternal confidence, she continued, 'Go and rescue that baby will you.' Then picking up a syringe she jabbed it into Denise's arm. 'This should stop any bleeding but we need

129

to get that placenta out now. Nurse Macpherson, get back here and see this labour through properly. Had you in all your glory forgotten about the third stage?'

Given the preceding drama, the after-birth sliding out into a kidney dish was something of an anticlimax. Meanwhile, Denise was getting her brain and body back, allowing her to operate normally once again.

'And I'll have that baby back now,' she said in a tone that meant business. 'I need a word with the wee love, even if he's given me such a hard time.'

Oliver, meanwhile, had stopped asking for more graph paper and started to chart something less meteoric whilst his girlfriend looked on as if he were drawing a masterpiece.

'Full throttle indeed!' chuckled Dr O'Reilly, stretching his neck and shaking his head. 'Must be a new gynaecological term. Still it seemed to do the trick. Wait till I tell my colleagues, and where did you say you trained, Nurse? I'd say you've the makings of a grand wee midwife there and, Sister,' he waved a spade-like hand under her nose, 'maybe you should look out gloves to fit smaller people.' He drifted off before Sister Flynn could tell him her theatre was the best equipped in Northern Ireland and that there were small gloves if people would only look.

Then, as if control might just be returning and within her reach, she looked at the contents of the kidney dish. 'That's good. A fine, healthy-looking placenta.' She put it aside almost tenderly. 'I'll take it to the sluice and look at it properly there. Of course, Nurse Macpherson,' her tone was withering, 'even though placentas can tell you a lot, you won't need to look at it since you're such an expert.'

'Och no, there's still one or two things I've to learn.' I thought this was rather daring but lacked the bottle to ask about the placenta's ultimate fate. There was a rumour that she dug them into her garden where the roses were apparently spectacular. By the same token, a bottle of enema soap might be handy for their green fly. A burnt pan, however, wasn't much use to anybody and would only put Sister Flynn into orbit if she found it.

One thing was plain. That pan needed shifting as quickly as Denise and her husband were now demanding to get out of labour ward.

12

RING A RING

In the small cubicle, home to so much of Denise's drama, a battalion of cleaners, strong in turban headscarved uniforms and Popeye arms, had moved in. They were scrubbing and hosing the place down as if to rid it of any lingering spirit.

I thought of asking if they'd any handy tips for dealing with incinerated articles but they were far too busy running to a Flynn schedule to stop. They'd shoved Denise's locker outside the kitchen and, stuck for any better idea, I pulled the pan out of its hiding place, stuffed it in a bag and shoved it into the locker just as Sister Flynn came round the corner.

'The porters must have forgotten to take the locker to the postnatal ward,' I said, hoping to sound less flustered than I felt, 'so I'll just take it up there before I go off duty.'

'Alright. That'd be good.' She sounded absentminded as she twitched her nose. 'It smells like a dead cat around here. It's probably a pair of oulde knickers I bet she hasn't washed since coming here. But I suppose her locker's her business.' She shook her head and sighed. 'You'd think a girl would have more pride about her wouldn't you?'

Before Denise's reputation could sink further, I grabbed my cloak, tore out of the labour ward and propelled the locker at a spanking rate, making its wheels bounce as I reached post-natal, where splashes of colour from floral bouquets at every corner made it a brighter world than the one I'd just left.

Here, patients converged in amiable groups, talking about their labours like athletes recovering from a major event. Even now, competition lingered as they outdid each other in tales of labour in all its merry facets, whilst their trophies lay in contented comas in cots beside their beds.

The less happy babies were in the nursery. It led off from the ward and William was standing outside it. With his nose pressed against the window he was gazing in at babies registering protest with such red faces and waving fists they made the room look like a shop stewards' convention. The locker wheels creaked and groaned as I trundled towards him but this new father didn't seem to notice.

'Where's your wife?' I asked, parking transport downwind.

'In that side ward,' William said, unable to take eyes away from the glass but thumb indicating a room opposite. 'They've given her a sedative. Thought she deserved it after all that hard work with her blood pressure and all.'

'Right. I'm just putting her locker back,' I said and went into a room so full of Denise's flowers their scent gave a competitive edge to the pan which I was now stuffing under my cloak. I thought Denise would be amused by its presence but I didn't want to disturb my star athlete, so I left the locker and tip-toed out.

'Congratulations, William,' I said but he just nodded. He too was in a different world – probably planning a pram on as grand a scale as his tractor.

Back along the corridor and heading for the Home, I met Father O'Patrick, who looked at me shifty-eyed. Maybe the pan bulge made him think this was a patient going in the wrong direction but he scurried away as if he didn't want to see anybody. This was a sentiment I shared completely as, top speed, I arrived at the pantry of our floor without meeting anyone else.

There was enough cleaning material here to scour Ulster so I set to, filling the sink with sufficient water and detergent to get a soap kitchen going and finding that water-play still held appeal with the pot bobbing about cheerfully, as if appreciating restoration.

'Brian and I are going to the Medical Ball.' Cynthia leant against the doorway. Her appearance was unexpected and could have been unwelcome had she not been so excited she didn't seem aware of either the pan or the suds.

'That's nice,' I said, sinking the pan. I was as amazed at the amount of bubbles enema soap could generate as at Cynthia's news that Dr Welch was such a fast operator.

'Yes, we're really excited.' She sighed happily, rubbing her London Hospital badge in such an absentminded way I nearly offered to show her how to clean it properly. 'So I'm going to go down town tomorrow after work to see if I can buy an evening gown. Something in gold I think.'

'Sounds your style.'

Ignoring sarcasm, she pressed on. 'I'm sick of the antenatal clinic and women just wanting to speak about their pregnancies, and I just know they won't want to hear anything about me, far less about a ball. It's next week so maybe and with a bit of luck we'll get a shift by then.'

I swished the water in triumph whilst keeping the pan down. This was my finest hour and not to be rushed. At length and as if careless I said, 'And by that time, I'll maybe have had a few more deliveries. I got my first one today.' I turned looking forward to seeing her reaction but she was gone and

I was speaking to myself.

Lisa came into the ward kitchen the next morning just as I was returning the pan, bright as a new sixpence, back to its cupboard. She wasn't singing and seemed worried.

'You wouldn't know anything about Denise's ring would you? Apparently it's gone missing.'

'She wasn't wearing it here,' I said. 'It's such a knuckle duster I'd have noticed it. Did she say where she thought it might be?'

Lisa spoke carefully. 'She's sure she put it in her locker but if she did it's not there now.' She gave a tuneless hum and clicked her teeth. 'The thing is, Jane, Sister Flynn said she saw you fiddling with the locker yesterday and you looked really flustered when she spoke to you about it.'

I was torn between guilt and outrage and a cold sweat gathered on my forehead. I had to swallow hard, eventually uttering, 'She's not actually accusing me of theft is she?'

'Well no, not really,' Lisa sounded miserable, 'but she couldn't have made it up about the locker. What were you doing with it?'

'Returning it to Denise, and I think I need to see her now. I'm really insulted. I've had a few things thrown at me in nursing but this has got to be the worst.'

I had tried to keep my voice down but

Oliver appeared as if at a reveille.

'Something up then?'

'Oh, not at all. I've just been accused of stealing, that's all. How dare they!' My voice trembled.

'How so?' He sounded clinically interested.

Lisa held up a placatory hand, 'I'm sure there's some misunderstanding and the ring'll probably turn up any minute now, but right now it's lost and Denise is really upset about it.'

'Not half as much as I am.' I was grim. 'Where's that bloomin' Sister?'

'Not on duty till later which is why she wanted me to speak to you. She wants it sorted out before she comes on duty. Said in a thing like this, time's of the essence.'

'She would and what does she think I have – a magic wand?' I figured a less disciplined person might have stamped her feet. I merely took a deep breath and gritted my teeth.

Plainly one for avoiding scenes, Oliver suddenly looked at his watch. 'Excuse me, but I need to do something. I'll be back in a jiffy and hopefully in time for a delivery.'

'You can have them all.' I was sour. 'Certainly I won't be around to stop you.'

Oliver made a line of his mouth and said as he left, 'Don't you be doing anything rash now.'

Lisa pulled on her curls. 'Ah, Jane, now, we're not accusing you of stealing. Things are always going missing between wards. I'm sure it'll turn up.' She seemed almost relieved when Dr O'Reilly's voice, full of urgency, called from the corridor, 'Prolapsed cord! Theatre! All Staff! Now!'

We poured into the corridor.

Had there not been an illustration in the midwifery textbooks I might have thought that this patient kneeling on a trolley on all fours and resting on her forearms was engaged in some form of Irish worship. Actually, this was the position needed to stop an umbilical cord coming before its baby. No wonder then that the mother was being whisked into theatre where a team was rapidly assembling, focussed on getting that baby out before the cord could block the life it had so far nourished.

In a previous existence I had been badly let down by the wilful vagaries of an operating table, determined to reach the ceiling despite my best efforts to get it do otherwise. I had learnt the hard way and now knew how to get instant co-operation as well as to do something clever and on the same lines as de-clutching. I leapt into theatre and got the table tilted before it had time to change its mind.

'Good girl,' approved Dr O'Reilly, 'nice light touch of feet there.'

I could have snapped, 'To match my fingers?' but there was enough drama going on to put any old and missing ring on the back boiler. Why on earth had I thought childbirth was a straightforward affair?

The atmosphere round the operating table reflected the silent tension of people having to deal with lives in the balance. Still, and compared to normal labour, a Caesarean section was quick and quiet. One scalpel cut was enough to produce a dazed-looking baby with such a startling immediacy I looked for a zip whilst wondering aloud why Sister Flynn wasn't promoting Caesareans as necessary for fine tuning the assembly line that was labour ward.

'It's dangerous. Needs a backup team,' Lisa explained, nodding at the anaesthetist and paediatrician, as engrossed in their work as a sewing bee. 'Patient might haemorrhage, baby could be affected by the anaesthetic and then there's all the problems of post-operative care and the discomfort of clips.' We watched as Dr O'Reilly, appearing to have swapped needlework skills for those of a joiner, stapled the final layer of skin on a now-flat abdomen.

'Just another wee miracle,' he said, pulling off his mask to allow a big beam to bring sunshine into the place. 'Thanks, Staff. Great team. Couldn't have done it without you.'

The baby was put in the quiet of an incubator whilst I was left to look after the patient until she was ready to go to the post-natal ward.

'Have you counted her jewels?' I had asked, but Lisa had just shaken her head and hurried away.

13

A BAG PACK

I was lying on my bed, considering the ceiling and hoping that, like this morning's patient, having my feet higher than my head would be beneficial.

There was a knock at the door, so timid it must be Marie.

'Come in!' I shouted, incapable of moving.

Marie sidled in, leaving the door open. She was carrying a piece of paper and gazing round-eyed as if legs resting halfway up the wall had mystic significance. Since there was nothing unusual about her looking anxious I presumed all was well but felt maybe I should explain the prone position.

'It's been a killer of a day. In fact, so bad that at one time I thought I should just pack my bags.'

Conversations with Marie tended to include some benign if unseen presence at her shoulder, since she usually kept darting her gaze over it as if to get reassurance before speaking. This time, however, there was no delay as she gasped, 'Sure, and is that not what Seonaid's actually doing? She's been given a terrible dressing down from Matron and had a warning.' She plucked at my arm then ran to the door. 'Come and see her, Jane. I've tried speaking to her but it's hopeless. She's one suitcase full already. It's a desperate situation so it is.'

I got up as quickly as throbbing corns would allow. 'You're beginning to sound like a proper Belfaster, come on.'

She put the paper down on my bedside locker.

'What's that?'

'Just a wee map of all the nearby churches, all denominations. You never know when it might come in handy.'

'Right now,' I said following her, 'if we'd the time.'

Seonaid was sitting on a suitcase, trying to shut it. Normally chaotic, her bedroom had progressed to a war zone. Her uniform, screwed into a ball, was jammed into a corner whilst books lay in a jumble beside her suitcase. Underwear, papers and dresses littered the floor whilst her cap had been flung in the waste paper bin. The only neat thing was a pair of tap dancing shoes tidily placed at her feet.

'I don't remember it being this difficult packing,' she said in a matter-of-fact sort of way, ignoring water overflowing from the hand basin. 'Marie, you're not missing any babbies are you? I think I maybe packed one in by mistake.' She sat on the lid, bounced on it, then sucking her lip in frustration, said, 'Come on and lend us your weight. I need to get it shut before midnight.'

'Indeed, and we will not, and that's not why we're here.' Marie's saints must have knocked off, leaving her surprisingly forceful. 'Jane, go and turn off that tap or we'll all drown. And would you look at the state of this room?' Tut-tutting, she started to pick things up from the floor, giving the proper respect to Seonaid's record book and a collection of shoes, the height of which made my sleeping bunion wake up and wince. If Seonaid was going to leave, she'd be better with walking shoes.

Outside these convent-like walls there was a different life, with the Falls Road traffic muttering about its business, whilst in the distance a recent fall of snow had covered the Belfast hills. Their forbidding countenances had been gentled into soft folds. When the weather was better we would have to go and explore them.

'Marie says you've been given a hard time

142

by Matron. What on earth's that about?'

Seonaid twiddled her toes, apparently a riveting sight. 'That oulde yoke Father O'Patrick went to visit her. He told her about me seeing Mrs Murphy and said I was interfering outwith the hospital and had persuaded her to have a sterilisation. Well, and much as I might have wanted to, I didn't. Anyway, I thought the Doc. would do a better job of it.'

'Did you tell her that?'

Seonaid shrugged. 'There wasn't much point. Sure I couldn't have interrupted her anyway – she's used to holding the floor. Remember when that Stormont fella came to make us take that oath of allegiance? I'm surprised she let him take centre stage and didn't knock him off his perch. Then, of course she wasn't best pleased either at a priest – a priest! – coming knocking and complaining at her door.' Seonaid scratched her head thoughtfully as if to prompt her memory. 'Oh yes! Then she said I shouldn't have been out in the Falls wearing the hospital uniform. The way she said it you'd have thought I'd gone down it naked!' She got up off the suitcase and stretched. 'Anyway, I could tell she was really pleased to get me into her office, gave her a chance to have a go about not buying her book as well.'

'She never mentioned that, did she?' Marie was scandalised.

'No. She just said she suspected I lacked application and would find the course difficult if I didn't use every learning tool available.' Seonaid's laugh was bitter. 'Well, I'm going to make it easy for myself and for her so I'm just going to leave – I can't be arsed with the hassle.'

She picked up a pair of tights and slung them in a bin. 'It's probably best this way anyway, saves time. There's plenty other things I could be doing. Now, would either of you have a spare suitcase there?'

'You didn't actually say you were leaving, did you?' I asked, crossing the room to look down on the street where a double-decker was waiting at traffic lights. They were a dull red in comparison to the colour of the bus which carried a sign advertising the cheering qualities of drinking Red Hand Guinness. A pint of it might have done some good to the sole passenger, a man wearing a flat cap and looking as dismal as Seonaid.

Beckoning the girls to come and have a look, I tapped the window and pointed. 'Quick! See him down there? He looks as if he's going nowhere.' Seonaid wrinkled her nose but came anyway. I nudged her. 'And that's where you'll be going if you leave. Honestly, Fitzy, I've never thought you'd be such a coward, but one measly little row and you're off packing your bags.'

Seonaid, continuing to look mulish,

stomped back to her packing but stopped when I added, 'At least she didn't accuse you of stealing.'

'Mother of God!'

At least I'd impressed Marie.

'What happened?'

I told them about the pan and the ring and how Sister Flynn, coming on duty, had taken me aside.

'And what did she say?' Marie had been rinsing a mug which was one of a pair Seonaid and I had bought in a small shop off Grosvenor Road. We'd wanted to own something with a homely touch. Being thick and having a florally design as busy as Seonaid's bedspread, it had fitted the bill. Marie was drying it as if in a trance.

'Give that to me. You'll polish off the design and I want to pack it.' Seonaid stretched out a hand and looked surprised when Marie batted it away.

'Go on with your wee story, Jane.'

'On our way to the office she asked me what I was doing with the locker and I was just about to tell her about the blessed pan, in front of everybody 'cause by that time I didn't care who heard, when who should appear but Oliver.'

Seonaid looked up in surprise,

'Oliver!'

Now she was interested.

I paused for a moment to look out the

145

window again and smiled, thinking back to the arrival of someone so unused to the novelty of bearing good news he was only able to pass it on in a casual way. The traffic lights had changed, the bus had moved on and I had an attentive audience.

'Come on, stop teasing us. What did he do?'

I blew out my cheeks as if recovering from a marathon, remembering Oliver whose leisurely entrance had been anything but athletic. 'Well, he just strolled in and said as if to the world in general and nobody in particular that the ring had been found. Denise's husband had taken it from the locker and brought it back home, as he was frightened it'd get lost. Denise was asleep when he took it so of course she wouldn't have known anything about it.'

Marie gave a little glad scream, which is what I might have done at the actual scene had I not wanted to see Sister Flynn's re-action. I was more sorry than amused to see her stretching her collar so that she could breathe easier. She was never going to apologise but had managed, 'That's good. Now carry on with your work. I think you should get the next delivery. It's due any minute.'

'So what did you say to Oliver?' Seonaid's return to curiosity was almost worth all that trauma.

'As soon as I could, I asked him how he'd

146

managed to come up with the goods. He said he'd phoned Denise's husband. It was the logical thing to do.' I didn't feel the need to say that that moment had been in the unlikely setting of the sluice where he'd followed me and got so close we were at squinting range.

'I knew you couldn't possibly have stolen the ring,' he'd said. 'For one thing, it would've been too small for you, and for another, your fingers seem to come in pairs. I can't think why you got yourself in such a silly situation.' Then, and so unexpectedly I hadn't a chance to get away, and with a bed pan handle sticking in my back, he'd leant over and stopped all talk with a kiss which had more power but much the same effect, I imagined, as a spin drier.

'I think you owed me that. Now we're even,' he'd said before walking off with the sly look of a successful poacher. Gratitude might be out the window but I thought people who stole such personal property might have some virtue.

'Well, all I can say is, good for Oliver. He certainly put you out of your misery. Though, honest to God, he doesn't look very much like a saviour. A puff of wind would blow him away.'

'It's not size that matters, Seonaid,' I said, giving her a hard look. 'There's some very small people around here who're givers too.'

Marie was nodding so vigorously it was amazing she didn't play her vertigo card. 'She's right. So let's put all our talk about leaving where it belongs,' she said, binning a scrap bit of paper, 'and get your stuff back where it should be. Now, where's your rosary?'

'When you put it like that, I suppose you're right.' Seonaid jumped up then pulled a face in her mirror. Marie and I exchanged hopeful grins as she gave a little jig. 'Ha! Maybe you're right and I should give Mider another wee try, but that Matron gets to you, you know. She's so sarcastic it gets under your skin.' Recovery beckoned with another pirouette. 'Let's go to the pictures. There's a good one on and I'll be in a better mood to sort this room out when we get back.'

'So what's the film about?' I asked as we headed downstairs,

'It's called *The Trap* and it's about a mute girl taken by a fur trapper to be his wife but I don't see that happening to any of us.'

'You'd be right there,' Marie agreed. 'I don't think we have any fur trappers in Ireland. Let's go!'

14

IT'S ONLY A GAME

'There's a letter here for you, Nurse Macpherson. I think it's from your mother.' Miss MacCready, splendid in pink, was overseeing her shiny-floored, people-free empire. 'I'll get it for you right now – you haven't heard from her for a while.'

She went into her booth and unlocked a small glass-enclosed cupboard, scrutinising the envelope with its spidery writing as she handed it over. 'Ah ha! Looks as if it's been written in a hurry, but maybe in Scotland copperplate's out of fashion. Not like us here where tradition's cherished.'

She might have launched into further Ulster wonders but for the sighting of our outdoor clothes. 'You're surely not going out tonight of all nights?'

As she wagged a finger, her bracelet jangled in tuneless reproach. 'D'ye not know there's a Rangers and Celtic football match on?'

'Here?'

Her look was pitying. 'No. Glasgow, of course.'

'It's only a game. Surely there can't be

much interest in Scots teams over here.' I doubted if Aberdeen's football team could raise a pulse beyond its city and wondered why somewhere across the water should be any different.

'Well, if you're not the innocent!' she marvelled. 'Over here support for the Old Firm's as powerful as religion. The pubs will be full of people watching the match.' I must've continued to look blank for she bunched her fist, slamming it into her hand and toed an imaginary ball. 'You'll be telling me next I'm a left-footer!' A few hairpins fell out as she shook her head and regained her balance. 'Ah, Nurse Macpherson, if only you knew!'

There were many things I didn't understand about living here, but I was beginning to realise why the entrance hall, guarded by its ardent nanny with her excessive care and opinions, was continually deserted. It might also explain why Seonaid, and even Marie, were now sprinting for the outside door.

'We're actually only going to the flicks and they're just down the road.' I was already hurrying after them but, because Miss Mac-Cready looked so anxious, I tried for a jokey, 'So in our case, it'll be best foot forward.'

'Just get home before the pubs close. Yez are very young and innocent girls. Still.' Her voice fluted after us.

'As if we'd go to a drinking place!' said

Marie, casting her eyes heavenward and belting her coat so tightly it was surprising she could breathe. 'That poor woman – she's such a worrier. She'll be dead before her time.'

Hunching her shoulders against a sleety shower blown down from the hills, she linked our arms, making us hurry as she towed us along. 'Come on, girls, it's freezing out here. I just hope the cinemas a bit warmer.'

'All that silent baptism's making you power crazy,' grumbled Seonaid but nevertheless sped up. 'Would you just get back into your cosy shell now.'

The picture house, untroubled by either fresh air or daylight, held in its plush, still atmosphere a hint of splendours past with its faded red curtains and well worn seats. Settling into the warm pleasant fug of a middle row, on sagging seats which creaked at every move, we concentrated on the film, aware there might be more excitement in the back row, but then the screen heroine upped the action, took an axe and aimed it at a block inches away from the sleeping hero.

Marie's arm gripped mine as she pulled herself to the edge of her chair, making it scream in alarm. Then, keeping her eyes glued to the screen, she whispered, 'D'ye think Seonaid would mind if I covered her record book? It's already beginning to look

151

tatty. Matron won't like that – or maybe she will. Give her another chance to call her into her office.' She paused to check the hero's head was intact. 'I'd say that was a rude awakening, and I've got some brown paper – if you like I could do yours as well.'

Drama might have been lost on her inside the cinema but it would have been hard to miss outside where, as we joined the audience emptying out onto the pavement, the sound of distant chanting floated down the Falls Road.

Next to us a woman in a sensible coat, the collar turned up against the cold, said to her companion, 'Ah, Patrick, can you hear that noise? The pubs must be closing. We'll have to hurry. We don't want to get caught up with any of those supporters. Come on!' She sounded worried but was unable to do anything, stuck as she was in a crowd that had the focus of a headless chicken.

Patrick flipped up his anorak hood, consulted his watch and clicked his teeth in annoyance. 'Your film went on too long. I should have slipped out before that soppy end. I was counting on getting you home and catching up with the football before it actually finished. I know it was just a friendly but still, I'd have liked to have seen Celtic thrashing Rangers.'

'I wouldn't be too sure of that.' A man,

muffled to the hilt with a blue and white scarf, spoke. 'Rangers are every bit as good, and don't you forget it. That crowd you're hearing,' he nodded in the direction of the distant shouts, 'will be cryin' 'cause they're backin' losers.' He was short and stocky and had a very thin wife hanging onto his arm.

The two women eyed each other speculatively whilst the men, preparatory to discussing the beautiful game, jutted their chins, squared their shoulders and moved closer to each other.

There was a library nearby capped with stone angels in meditative poses. They looked down on a stirring restlessness. It wasn't a worry for them, but it certainly was for those caught in the middle of it and not appreciative of the finer points of football. Still, it seemed, there was a growing number who were. Each an expert on football and its players, they began to contribute. Influenced by so much sporting chat the formless crowd began to move into combative lines.

That sneaky snow-laden wind tugged at coats and pulled on scarves whilst a bus splashed past, soaking those on the outside of the pavement. As sides were becoming clearer the crowd's murmur grew in disharmony. Women plucked at sleeves as if to hold back action but such restraint was misinterpreted. Jostling broke out. A bottle crashed to the ground, followed by the ominous sight of somebody picking it up and brandishing it. There was a pause whilst the crowd, like some animal suddenly trapped and preparing to lash out, held its breath. Then, into the silence a scream speared the night.

'Ah, stop now!' It was Seonaid who, covering one eye with one hand was holding up the other in a halt position. 'Everybody! Me lenses! I've lost a contact lens. Don't any of yez move or you might stand on it!'

All eyes swivelled towards a small figure squatting on all fours frantically patting the street as if she were soothing it. 'I can't afford to lose it. If you just give me a minute I'm bound to find it – it can't be far away.'

As still as the statues above, the crowd stayed put, fixed on the diminutive figure with the same attention as the hero had given the axe-wielding heroine, until, unable to contain himself, Patrick stepped forward. 'I'll give you a hand.'

'Don't move!' yelled the thin wife. 'Or you'll stand on it.'

'That's right,' approved Patrick's wife, 'with feet as big as your mouth, how could you miss?'

Abashed, he melted into the background.

Carefully I hunkered down beside Seonaid. 'You'll never find it,' I muttered, aware of the crowd on either side, 'but at least I know how Moses felt or,' I winced, feeling gravel on my palms, 'maybe even a penitent.'

'There's more religion about you than you let on,' Marie whispered as she joined us, 'but it'll be a miracle if we get anything but broken glass and filthy frozen hands. Sacred Heart, I can't believe I'm doing this – and would you just listen to that supporters' noise coming near? We're going to get caught up in even more trouble. What's wrong with specs anyway – at least they'd be easier to find. Now, Seonaid, where did you see it last?'

Undaunted, Seonaid continued patting, apparently not only blind but now deaf to the sound of chanting coming nearer.

'For God's sake, Wee Doll, would you find that lens,' called someone in a resigned fashion. 'Then we can all go home. We're beginning to freeze.'

The wind was also searching, looking for small, unprotected spaces and gleefully invading sites of special interest. It had found a resident spot in the small of my back and made me shiver and wonder if the possible signs and symptoms of hypothermia could be linked to fear. If Seonaid's search proved fruitless maybe we'd all be found in the morning, frozen to the spot, suitable candidates to join the angels crowning the library.

Then, like a goal scorer, Seonaid gave a triumphant cry. 'Found it!' She got up, holding her palm steady with her other hand, turning in a circle and supposing that everybody could see a minute piece of plastic. 'There! I knew if I just kept trying it'd give itself up. Thanks, everybody. Now we can all go home.'

'Thank God for that,' said the man in the blue and white scarf, stamping on his feet to restore circulation. 'You wouldn't by any chance be a nurse?'

'Yes. Why?'

'It's the bossiness. But you'd better hurry on up the road. By the sound of that pub crowd, they're not in the mood to be stopped by anybody, least of all a wee nurse like you.' He tapped her lightly on the shoulder then, nudged by his wife, hurried away.

Not to be outdone, Patrick spoke up. 'We could come with you – make sure you get home all right, we're going that way anyway.' He shook himself as if limbering up but Marie pointed to his wife. 'Look at your wife now. She's just flagged down that taxi. You'd better hurry or you'll miss it.' She made a prayerful gesture and added, 'Don't you be worrying about us, there's three of us and with the help of the good Lord that makes four.'

Not one to query divine intervention, Patrick hurried away.

A ragged moon had freed itself from the tethering murk and now shone with a watery light as if beginning a new elemental chapter. Still it was cold, and in its rawness all appetite for blood sport seemed to have evaporated. Desultory chat broke out as the crowd started to disperse, with people hunched in universal complaint about the weather as they either caught buses or walked off, the sound of musical chanting apparently no longer a crowd puller.

'I haven't much of an ear for it,' I said, lengthening my stride, 'but that singing's flat. God's choir boys they ain't, and though I don't see how we can avoid them, I really, really don't want to meet them.'

The sound of a bottle landing gave its own discordant pitch. 'D'you hear that? Sounds as if the game hasn't gone the choristers' way.'

'And you sound as if you'd have liked them to win,' said Marie, sounding surprised.

'I don't know who they are but it's only a game,' I shrugged. 'I don't understand the big deal and frankly I don't care. It wasn't ever such an issue in that sinful city where I trained.'

For a moment, the Falls Road held the emptiness of an alien planet. Quite often and at any time through the day, tank-like prams stuffed with children would be pushed along the street by harassed-looking women, heading out on some urgent mission in thin slippers and curlers anchored by faded headsquares. Now there was nothing but a vocal blob weaving towards us and

157

looming larger and getting louder. Even though Bostock House was near, its distance was beginning to seem insuperable.

'If we hurry we could beat them to it,' Marie quavered, 'or maybe they'll just pass us by. It'll look bad if we cross the road just in front of them.'

A figure detached himself from the crowd and, picking up speed, weaved towards us. With a fine disregard for melody he yelled, 'Look! Women!'

As if it would give us immunity and clinging onto her rosary, Marie squeaked, 'Girls!'

'I wish I'd on my Doc Martens,' said Seonaid. 'I'm thinking they'd be very useful right now. Jasus! I should have left when Matron gave me the chance.'

When I was applying to Belfast to do my training for a bit of adventure and change, I hadn't quite bargained on this level of excitement. Now I was gripped with the same regret as Seonaid. The crowd coming towards us looked so ferocious I thought we might be about to jettison maternity for eternity.

'Come on! Let's just cross. Now!' Seonaid grabbed our arms, dragging us to the edge of the pavement.

'Watch!' I cried. A van was hurtling towards us. Then over the sound of the crowd came the screech of its tortured brakes, followed by a terrible silence.

15

MISSION VAN

The van had slewed round. Marie was crying, which seemed unnecessary since Seonaid, apparently sound in wind and limb, was asking the driver what had kept him.

With timing better than in any B-movie the driver had cranked down his window, saying in a familiar voice and with the cool grace of a man accustomed to walking on water, 'Hop in!'

I never thought I would be so pleased to see Raymond – or his old beat-up truck, even if since our last trip it had acquired a large crack that fractured the windscreen. The pink sticking plaster attempting to cover it added a rakish look, but still I thought it had more appeal than a Rolls-Royce.

The roar of the crowd faded as, scrambling aboard, we slammed the door behind us. 'Let's go then,' he cried, throwing a devil-may-care arm out the window to slap the van side by way of encouragement.

We roared full throttle down the Falls Road. Cautiously, I felt around. Apart from football supporters robbed of their quarry something else was missing. 'It's too comfortable in the back. What have you done with the pelvis?'

'Oliver took it. He and his girlfriend were planning some study and thought it might come in handy.'

'I thought they'd gone their separate ways,' said Seonaid. Sitting in the front, she had assumed the brace position. 'And I see from the side we're on, you're practising for driving in France.' She gripped her knees. 'Personally, in case anybody feels like asking, I'd just like to survive here in the Oulde Country.'

'Ah, don't you be worrying now. This way makes cornering easy.' Raymond pulled so hard on the steering wheel the van began to list in such a fashion it seemed impossible not to capsize. 'Oliver and Bridie have made it up – seems she'd second thoughts after watching him play a big part in a recent delivery.'

'She should have seen him playing an even bigger one in the sluice,' I could have said had I not suddenly been jammed into Marie who was squeaking enough to show she was still alive. The van righted itself in time for another corner.

'Look,' boasted Raymond, 'Grosvenor Road.'

'I know,' said Seonaid. 'We're so close to the road sign, I could have read it without

160

my lenses and isn't this the road that takes you to the main hospital and Maternity entrances? Since we girls are meant to take the tradesman's entrance we'd hardly know this was here – not unless we were on a special tour.' She sounded full of disapproval.

Wheels spun and we swayed as if in a drunken waltz. Then, making a crazy burst along a straight stretch, we screamed along before two-wheeling into a smaller road fronted by square buildings. They'd a liverish colour and were so utilitarian and uniform-looking we must have reached the hospital complex. With a sigh of relief Seonaid read out a sign on the first building. 'Maternity! Well thank the Lord for that.'

'Hitherto an unseen treasure,' I said, taking in high, mean-eyed windows and a main entrance door beside which were larger, crowd-repelling double ones. 'They must be for the ambulances. With style like yours, Raymond, you could drive through them without breaking speed. Say we're an emergency.'

Raymond laughed and took his foot off the pedal. 'Three ladies in labour? I don't think so.' The van, seeming pleased to have a rest, coughed then shuddered to a halt. Steam issued distress signals from under the bonnet but Raymond ignored them. He pointed to a block, squat and toad-like on its own, a few metres further along. 'I can let you off now.

That's the district unit. It's got a back door to the Home so you can get in easy enough. Nobody'll notice. Nurses come and go all the time.'

Seonaid was suspicious. She tried to wipe the steam off the window but it was all on the other side. Tut-tutting, she craned her neck to look out. 'How d'you know?'

Raymond splayed his fingers, banged them on the wheel then stretched back in a relaxed way. 'It'd be odd if I didn't. Our medical residence's just behind the medical school there.' He nodded at a big complex opposite the unit and separated by a grassed area with trees moving dark shadows over it. 'The District midwives are going out at all times – we see them on their bikes during the day and they get taxis if they've to go out at night. They tell me babies come at all times but maybe, being a mere medic, I'm just making an assumption and I'm sure you'll tell me if I'm wrong.'

Whilst Seonaid exuded silence, Marie was perking up and looking about with the lively interest of a keen student. 'So this is where we'll be coming if we get through First Part Mider, and I suppose that adjoining shed there's where they keep the bicycles. I've heard they're the best bit about District. Just think, girls! The freedom of the road with all the traffic stopping to let you through!' She whirred her thumb as if already ringing her bell. 'It must be like flying.'

'You might remember that, Raymond, the next time you put the foot down.'

I'd never seen Seonaid so sour but suddenly she started, then pointed at somebody peering through the shed window. 'Hey! That looks like Margaret.'

'That's because it is Margaret. I wonder what she's doing there.' Margaret's furtive skulking was making me especially curious.

'Let's go and find out.' Seonaid made to get out but Raymond stayed her. 'Just before you go, will you tell me if you'll come to the Medical Ball? I did ask you before but you didn't get back to me. It should be good craic but I need to know now so that I can get tickets.' His open, farmer's face was clouded with anxiety.

Stuck in the back, Marie and I could do nothing other than affect a huge interest in Margaret. Raymond didn't seem to mind an audience but Seonaid wasn't playing, saying nothing, chewing her lip and tapping her toes together by way of showing she'd been struck dumb. Tension in the van grew. Marie nudged me. We held our breath.

There wasn't enough room for her to sit cross-legged, but as it was Seonaid, her arms folded across her chest gave a good impression of a leprechaun deep in thought. At last she managed, 'Ach, I'm not sure now – I need time to think, and would you look at Margaret – you'd think she was trying to break into that shed.'

Marie, growing restless, leant forward and, placing a timid hand on Seonaid's shoulder, said, 'Would you stop changing the subject? Raymond here's just after helping us through a sticky patch. I don't know what we'd have done if he hadn't come along, so at the very least you should be grateful, and, as for going to a Ball, why would you not want to go to one – it's yourself that loves dancing.'

'She's right. Just go,' I put in. 'Come on, Seonaid, we're all waiting, and more to the point, we're in one bit. There was a while I thought we'd have to be scraped off the Falls.'

Seonaid sighed, threw up her hands then said in an exasperated way, 'Oh, alright then, but if I don't enjoy myself, I'll just come home.'

'You won't have far to go,' said Raymond, a wide smile throwing him out of nonchalance mode. 'It's going to be in the medical school. Oh, it'll be a grand affair alright. You won't be thinking of leaving till the last waltz.'

'And I won't have to pay for the ticket?'

'Certainly not!' Raymond sounded affronted.

'Well, OK then,' said Seonaid with a sigh. 'Thanks for the lift and come on, girls or we'll miss Margaret.'

We tumbled out. Raymond, apparently unfazed by Seonaid's ingratitude, slammed a valedictory whack on his trusty steed then roared off tooting the horn. 'He's going to wake everybody up with that racket,' Seonaid complained. 'God! He's so unaware. I wish I'd never said I'd go to the ball.'

'Oh well, you have now.' I was philosophical. 'What's wrong with him anyway. He's so cheery and I bet he'll make a good doctor. And as for the ball, Cynthia's going and she'll keep him in order as well as everybody else. You never know, Seonaid, if you're not careful, you might just enjoy yourself. Now, where's Margaret?'

We turned to look then jumped in fright on two accounts. Firstly on being startled by someone who had unexpectedly arrived and secondly on who that someone was.

'What was that terrible racket and what do you suppose you're doing out here at this time of night?' asked Matron.

We could have asked her the same question. Was she not supposed to be tucked up in bed contemplating its virginal eighteen-inch sheet turnover, figuring how to get more carbolic into the medical system She was the last person we – and Seonaid in particular – needed to see but it would have taken a brave heart to ask what a Matron was doing out at this time of night, fresh as the approaching morning but twice as frosty.

'Well?'

Rabbit-like, we were caught in the search-light of her enquiry. We scuffled our feet on a pavement lined with small shrubs. They looked sickly but strong enough in the biting wind to whip our ankles as if urging escape.

'I'm waiting for an explanation.'

I heard Seonaid draw breath. Aware that she was in no mood to receive another lecture I kicked her hard whilst Marie gave a pitiful whinny. The moon, as if sensing trouble, hid behind a curtain of cloud, leaving us ghastly-looking in the colour-robbing street lights.

'And if it's not yourself, Matron, but isn't it grand to be seeing you.'

Margaret emerged from the shadows. With her slightly bowed head and clasped hands she wore the mien of some saintly academic out on a spiritual voyage whilst her voice had the husky quality of sweet reason. 'We've all just been taking a stroll before going back to study.'

She was wearing a cloak that she flung out in an all-embracing gesture. 'Were we not just saying, girls, that a little fresh air's the very thing to help clear the brain?' We nodded as if hypnotised whilst Margaret pressed on. 'Of course we could have gone down the Falls Road, but sure it's full of revellers after watching the football and we

166

knew you wouldn't want us putting our lives at risk amongst such crowds.'

Resistant to the most beatific of smiles, Matron was more intent on regaining ground.

'Never mind the Falls Road. I wouldn't be here had it not been for that dreadful car noise. It must have wakened the entire district.' She gestured at the surrounding buildings that were as alive as a morgue. 'This is a hospital area not a fairground. I must have the driver's name and you girls must know him.'

Margaret looked surprised. 'Well I certainly don't but of course there's a medical residency around here and he may well be one of their students, and you know how thoughtless they can be.' She smiled indulgently. 'Their training hasn't the same discipline as ours so I suppose we shouldn't expect too much from them, eh? Now, girls!' She stretched her arms then, pulling the cloak close, spoke with the confidence of a theatre Sister after a successful operation. 'If you'll excuse us, Matron, we really need to be going back inside. Study calls, and maybe you too should be coming inside with us. It's *really* bitter out here and we wouldn't want you to be getting your death of cold.'

'Oh, wouldn't we?' muttered Seonaid as we scurried away from the battlefield and after our leader.

'Hey, Margaret, we can't thank you enough. You really saved our bacon there,' I said as we tumbled into the lift, 'but don't tell us you just happened to be out in a freezing cold night just for the good of your health.'

Margaret blushed, then put the lift button on hold. 'No. In fact, it's a good thing you came along when you did. I wouldn't have wanted Matron asking me too many questions. There's something I've got to tell you.' In a shame-faced way she bowed her head, 'I've a really big problem...'

16

A LOSING GAME

'So how're ye doin'?'

Last night seemed like a dream with Seonaid in skipping mode, looking refreshed and ready for any kind of action whilst Marie had the bright, optimistic look that only a morning of clandestine christenings could offer.

We were passing through the main hall where the receptionist was sorting the mail with the random accuracy of a paper dart thrower. I wasn't looking for letters today, unlike Cynthia who was hovering nearby and looking unusually humble.

'Hello there, Cynthia. You're up early. I thought you'd a day off.'

'Just checking if I've mail and can get it.' She raised her eyebrows as Miss MacCready ignored her and continued her postal sorting duties.

Marie, plainly not as interested as Cynthia in mail matters, had been fidgeting beside us and could contain herself no longer.

'I've got some big news and I think it'll please you, Cynthia,' she burst out.

Seonaid and I were horrified. Surely she wasn't going to split on Margaret, and to Cynthia of all people? We hoped for restraint but Marie, cheeks pink and eyes sparkling, was unstoppable. 'Great news!' She glanced over, daring us to interrupt, then pressed on. 'Seonaid's been asked to the Medical Ball! One of the students asked her last night. Isn't that grand?'

Her happiness barely registered on Cynthia. Keeping her eyes trained on Miss Mac-Cready, she said, 'Oh, a student!' Her sniff was dismissive. 'Well that's jolly nice for you I'm sure and of course I'll see you there, but we'll be at the doctors' table.'

Seonaid was less than enthusiastic as she shrugged. 'The food better be good no matter what table we're on. Anyway, I'm not that keen to go but these two yokes persuaded me.' She prodded us hard. 'So now I'll have to find something to wear and I don't suppose Raymond will want to fund that.'

Marie herself might not be going to the Ball but she was plainly enjoying its prospect. 'And have you got your dress, Cynthia?'

'Actually, that's why I'm here. The one I was telling Jane about is a little out of my budget range. I've phoned Daddy to ask for help buying it and I'm waiting for a cheque to arrive any moment.'

'So no gold number yet then?' I asked.

'No.' The reply was flat and since the receptionist now seemed to have gone blind as well as deaf, Cynthia flung her hands up in exasperation and said, 'I don't know what I've to do to get noticed around here but at least I've got a day off.' She raised her voice fractionally, aiming it at the back of Miss MacCready's top knot. 'So I've plenty of time to wait for when the mail eventually gets sorted. I'm going to take a seat, no matter how long it takes.'

We left her sitting on one of the window benches at the front entrance. She'd crossed her arms and fixed a steely glare upon the receptionist who was now slowing down to a snail's pace and complaining about how difficult certain letters were to decipher.

'By the time Cynthia gets that letter, the Medical Ball will have been and gone,' I said as we headed for work. 'Miss MacCready shouldn't be giving her such a hard time. You could see she's desperate for that letter – I kind of feel sorry for Cynthia.'

'Me too, and for Margaret as well. Sure an' I never thought I'd ever say that – they've always seemed such copers.' Marie was astonished.

Seonaid put in, 'You're right. On top of all that stuff last night, Margaret certainly gave us a big surprise. It's the last reason I expected her to be where she was, still less that she needed help and we kind of owe her for sorting out Matron.' She had a speculative look. 'Jane, with all your tales about gadding round the countryside, you'd be up for helping, wouldn't you?'

'Of course, but we won't need an audience. Maybe an ambulance though.' I turned to Marie. 'What d'you say we Cinderellas have a trial run the night of the ball when everybody's attention's taken up with all the excitement of that?'

Ruminating on Margaret's secret I got to the labour ward, where in the absence of any labouring patients, Sister Flynn was scribbling out the week's duty rota.

'You're not here,' she said, twirling the pencil, 'you're to go to the Special Nursery.'

171

I must have looked surprised as I turned on my heel, because she added irritably, 'Not right now, you eejit, next week. How many deliveries have you now?'

'Four.'

'You've done well then for this being your first time here.' From her dry tone I presumed she meant numerically. 'And I hope you've got your witness book handy. I don't remember signing it at all.'

'I'll bring it in, Sister. It's not quite to hand.'

How true! In all my post-delivery excitements I'd forgotten this essential detail. I wasn't even sure where the book was. It must be somewhere here. But where?

It was nerve-wracking enough going to be cast loose in the nursery with its frail little passengers, but without finding the book and getting it signed I wouldn't be going anywhere. I cast my mind desperately to where I'd last seen it.

I went into the kitchen and pretended to have a purge on cleaning whilst, with an ever increasing panic, scouring only the upboards. From its throne of a shelf my pan glinted at me, at least providing evidence that my time in the labour ward hadn't entirely been wasted. But that was of little comfort as I foraged further. I was convinced the book must be here but to no avail. Plainly the dratted thing was well and truly lost.

17

NO JOKE

'Mercy! You'd think a bomb had hit the place.' Lorna, our class's cheerful cherub, stuck her head round my bedroom door.

I was especially pleased to see her. Compared to Seonaid's frenetic approach to life and Marie's doom-laden prognostications, she managed to combine a sense of fun with that of orderly calm. She said, 'And I thought only Seonaid could create this level of havoc. Have you been counting all your earthly possessions?'

'Yes. They're all there bar my record book,' I said, gesturing at the covered floor space. 'I was sure I had it here, but apparently not and the trouble is that, having no patients around today, that bloomin' Sister Flynn's been chasing me all over the place about it. Eventually I had to say I'd a bad dose of the curse to get me off duty. At least that got me out of her way. I've been turning this place upside-down ever since, but with no luck.' I gave a huge sigh. 'I don't know what I'm going to do. My life seems full of complications other people manage to avoid. I bet you haven't lost your book.'

Lorna came into the room. She looked like a cocoa advertisement in her red flannel dressing gown and her hair pigtailed down the back. Even having her perching on one cheek and twinkling at me from the end of my bed made me feel better.

'Well no I haven't but maybe there's something in the wind. Same as you, Seonaid's lost her book and she's turning her room upside-down too, though in her case it's hard to see the difference. Now you, Nurse Mac, are usually more organised. You've been clocking the deliveries too. You won't want to have to go through all that again, will you?' She stirred a pile of clothes with a desultory foot then turned with the look of a kindly advisor. 'Now! Where did you see it last?'

'If I knew that, we wouldn't be having this conversation.'

Lorna looked thoughtful. 'One way or another you three always seem to be up to something. You make the rest of us look very dull. And where's Marie, anyway? She might know. She's always going on about keeping it in a safe clean place. She even makes me nervous.' She put her hands, palms up, as if warding off evil.

'Probably taken it to church to make sure it gets plenty blessings. Marie's such a worrier I haven't told her about the book. Blast! What a waste of time. I've spent all evening looking for the...' I felt a swear coming on but Lorna might not approve, 'darn thing.'

'It's bound to turn up. You look shattered. Why don't you just go to bed? Everything seems better in the morning.' There was a hint of mischief as she added, 'If you'd like, I'll put in a special wee prayer for you tonight.'

'It'll need to be a big one,' I said and threw a slipper at her. It missed and caught Cynthia as she barged in. Dressed in gold, she must eventually have had success with the postal service.

'Oh, I say!' For a moment she looked taken aback, then heading for some space, located a bare bit of floor and gave a twirl.

'What do you think?'

'You'll certainly be noticed,' said Lorna, 'and the colour's just you.' Cynthia pursed her lips, puffed her cheeks and pulled in her stomach. 'You don't think it's too tight?'

'No, it's fine – just remember not to bend,' I said and went to the door to look out. 'Just checking for the footmen and carriage.'

Cynthia cast a reproachful look. 'I've never thought of myself as Cinderella, Jane, and as you're not going to the Ball, at least I'll be able to tell you about it. I must say,' she preened in front of the mirror, 'I'm getting excited about going. I can't wait for tomorrow night.'

Lorna wound her pigtail into a halo, stood

up and stretched. 'Well us poor Cinderellas'll be waiting eagerly for it too.' She
cupped her hand to her ear. 'And I'm thinking I already hear the sound of the carriage
wheels being pumped up.' She turned at the
door as she left, then added, 'I heard your
man Oliver telling his friend Raymond he
wasn't going. It was too expensive.'

'He's not my man,' I said automatically.

'So I heard,' laughed Lorna and left,
closely followed by Cynthia, suddenly so
overtaken by getting her dress and its trial
run she said she too had to get to bed.

The following morning, Marie called. Eyes
shining and ready for the day, she seemed
surprised by my surly responses and reluc-
tance to get out bed. It was safer tucked
under the blankets and not confronting the
major problem of book loss.

'Aren't you going on duty this morn?'

Not bothering to open my eyes, I groaned
and rolled over. 'It's hardly worth it. I've lost
my record book and Old Flynn's chasing me
for it. Without it, I'd bet she won't let me
near any patient.' I gave a despairing sigh. 'I
just don't know where I put it so right now
I've got a major problem.'

'Ah!'

Something in her tone made me open my
eyes.

'Both you and Seonaid left yours lying on

176

a table in the dining room so I took them both away and covered them.' She waved two brown paper-covered books under my nose with the flourish of a conjuror. 'I hope you didn't mind but I was worried about them.'

'Not half as worried as me,' I said, getting out of bed and shaking her with, under the circumstances, commendable restraint. 'Marie, you'll be the death of us. I know Seonaid's been hunting high and low for her book. Just you go and tell her about your good deed before she commits suicide.'

'That's a mortal sin.'

'So's murder. Away you go!'

With all the reverence of handling state jewels I placed the book in front of Sister Flynn. She, pen hovering, scrutinised it before eventually scribbling her signature in the appropriate boxes.

'I've to write a report about you too,' she sighed, scratching her brow and looking harassed. 'So you can expect a visit to Matron's office. Now I must dash, I'm late.' With that she sped off probably to drum up custom from the antenatal ward.

I spent the rest of the week worrying about an imminent summons. I kept well out of Flynn's way and tried not to think of a likely and unpleasant encounter heading mine. You didn't go to Matron's office for congratulations though Margaret alleged she often popped in for a pleasant chat. I couldn't imagine ever doing that but maybe it was Margaret's idea of a joke. Sometimes Irish humour had me foxed.

I wondered where I'd gone so wrong that my next destination was going to be Matron's office. Was this a formality before a departure? I'd just arrived! And it was no good telling anybody else about it. Despite what Lorna said, when it came to drama, our group was competitive.

Then, eventually and on my last day, I blurted out my anxiety to Lisa who, in the absence of any action in labour ward, was brewing up in its kitchen.

She looked surprised then amused. 'Ah sure she'd only be joking. Don't you be thinking she's that bad. Under that bib and tucker beats a fun-loving heart. You should have come to me sooner and I'd have put you out of your misery. You've been grand here, so you have. I've even heard her say so.' She handed me a cup of coffee black enough to have pace-making qualities. 'Here! Swallow this, it'll do you good. I can't think why you've been worrying – save that for the Nursery.' Then she went off into the corridor, strains of 'Do What You Do Do Well' floating gently in her wake.

18

DRIVING LESSONS

Only Seonaid and Cynthia were going to the Ball, but our corridor had all the excitement of a drama unfolding. Everybody, bar Margaret, was keen to watch the girls getting ready. She was cloistered in her room and readying for an alternative pursuit of something equally exciting if different.

'It's maybe my imagination but I think you've grown,' said Marie as Seonaid, dressed in red, pirouetted in front of us with the grace of a flame.

'It's a piece,' she said, patting the extra inches of hair, 'and I'm praying it doesn't come off, at least until we start dancing. Then if it does, I'll pretend it doesn't belong to me.' She thought for a moment. 'I could put the breeze up Raymond. Scream and say it's a rat.' Her heels pumped and she gave another twirl.

'Sounds as if it's going to be a fun night then, especially as you'll be putting the guy so much at ease. And what about you, Cynthia? Can we help you fix anything?' asked Lorna, already in her dressing gown.

'Jolly nice of you to offer, but no thanks, I think I'll manage,' said Cynthia, using a jewelled clip to harpoon her hair into a French plait. She sounded unusually anxious. 'But you'd tell me if I didn't look alright, wouldn't you?'

I thought she looked splendid and said so.

'I'd say she was like Brittania on Speed,' whispered that naughty Lorna, watching a reassured Cynthia take off in a vapour of Madame Rochas. 'But maybe that's what that Brian Welch needs. She might speed him up if his brain can make the connections. He's as slow as a two-toed sloth. I once saw him in the antenatal ward lengthen his stride. I almost put it in the report book.'

Marie gave a little cry. 'You're cruel, Lorna, so you are. Did you not see how happy she looked? I think it's grand that he asked her.'

'Ah! But he didn't. She asked him – bought his ticket too.'

I was stunned. Cynthia was renowned for her thrift. I said, 'Maybe she's changing. I'll test her. Next time I ask her for coins change for the phone, I'll expect her to give them without asking to see the colour of my money first.'

'Now you'd be asking for a miracle there but here's one to be going on with,' Lorna said, turning to Seonaid. 'You've grown by another six inches, I'd say.'

Seonaid teetered past. Despite all her complaints about Raymond, she looked excited. 'Feet killing me already. I'll never last the night. Expect me back before midnight.'

'No matter how early that is, it'll be after I'm in bed,' said Lorna, stifling a yawn. 'Some of us need our beauty sleep. Goodnight, folks.'

Once everyone was gone we fished Margaret out of her room. She was dressed in enough protective gear to withstand nuclear fallout and was highly nervous.

'I see Seonaid and Cynthia weren't the only ones getting dressed up for tonight,' I said, taking in the goggles and shin guards. 'They're wonderful gauntlets – they look as if they belong to a biker.'

'They do,' Margaret replied briefly. 'They're my brother's. He said I'd need them if I was biking round the district.'

We were about to help Margaret deal with her big problem and she sounded despairing. 'Only you girls know I can't ride a bike. I was trying to get one to practise on when you appeared.'

As secrets go, I thought it a pretty poor effort, but it was certainly true she needed that particular skill to move onto Second Part Midwifery, when we'd need to get about the streets. I'd never thought it was an unusual talent but it had certainly reduced

Margaret to something resembling humility. Who'd have thought it! If we'd been surprised earlier by her embarrassed admission, now we were more amazed when she said that even her brother didn't know.

'How did you manage to keep it a secret?' I asked.

Her shrug conveyed a world-weary disdain for the question, whilst hinting at a score unsettled. 'He was bigger than me and always grabbed the bike first. Whenever I tried to have a go, he'd shove me off. After a while, I just stopped trying.'

'You've had a serious omission in your educational development,' I said, enjoying this brief spell of superiority, 'and Marie and I are here to help fill the gap. It's actually dead easy. We'll show you. So let's go. Thank goodness Jo's on duty. We'll get the bike shed key from reception without the MacCready third degree.'

Outside, music floated faintly from the direction of the medical residence with a distant burst of laughter, making the atmosphere a bit more cheerful than it had been on our last visit. Light spilt onto the grassed area. Shrubs hunkered together like gossips discussing the attendees whilst the occasional couple, bent on intimacy amongst the trees, looked for as much privacy as us, their smothered giggles somehow involving us in their conspiracy.

I turned the key in the bike shed lock, swung the door open and saw a line of bikes. They weren't quite original boneshakers, but as I handled one, quickly realised were faithful to the original in terms of weight.

'Choose your weapon!' At least their tyres were rubber and they had three speed gears. However, Margaret was looking so apprehensive it was doubtful she appreciated such refinements. 'It's all to do with confidence. Isn't that right, Marie?'

'Oh, surely. Come on, Margaret, it's only a bicycle.' Marie wheeled one to the door. 'Is this one not just waiting for you?' She patted the seat in an encouraging way, her smile at its most seraphic. 'If you get on, we'll both hold it. Come on now, that's a good girl.' Marie's wheedling tone should have had Margaret doing a saddle vault but she just stood stock still, staring – even trembling. Her gauntlets waved in the air.

'I can't do it, I really can't.' Her voice verged on hysteria whilst she stood bracing herself as if preparing to fight off an attacker.

'Oh, just get on!' I said, throwing patience out the window. It was cold standing about and I could have been in bed instead of out here in a whistling wind, gripping onto the handlebars of a lead weight, trying to convince somebody that getting onto something they were likely to fall off was a progressive move. 'Look you can't possibly come to harm – not with us here.'

Something between a cry and a snort betrayed Margaret's doubt, but at last, grabbing Marie by one shoulder she climbed on, then rally-racer style gripped the handlebars, feet tip-toed to the ground. Now that we'd become stabilisers it was our turn to brace ourselves. Margaret's weight might have been an advantage in sumo wrestling but not for this activity.

'Don't let go!' The voice was muffled amongst enough scarves to bandage her into a mummy. 'And where's the brakes?'

'You'll never find them with these goggles on. Take them off and I'll look after them,' I offered.

'Well take good care of them. Anyway, somebody might recognise me,' she bleated.

'Oh for goodness sake, who'd be interested? There's nobody around. Look! The road's empty – perfect for a maiden launch. Marie and I'll wheel you down a bit so that you get the feel of things. Try putting your feet on the pedals. That's right. Come on, you can do this.'

With the goggles removed, a pale sheen of sweat could be seen on her forehead, but the long road beckoned and it wasn't time to lighten up. 'Good heavens, Margaret. You don't want Cynthia thinking she's got one over you.'

'She already has. She's at the Ball.'

Who'd have thought Margaret possessed such a weeny voice?

'Well, we're not either, so how about doing something constructive. Let's go.'

Marie and I, like frail tugs trying to guide a liner, set off down the road, our ship making us veer so crazily our muscles strained and protested as if they were being pulled apart.

'Has anybody seen the harbour master?' I asked, longing for a straight course.

'Ah, now, stop that and your laughing or we'll all end in the bushes,' Marie reproached and suppressed a giggle.

I'd been relying on her to be Captain Sensible and now here she was putting concentration in jeopardy.

Margaret's jaw set. She clamped her feet on the pedals then started to turn them in the ponderous way of a paddleboat.

'That's right, keep going.' Encouraging and upping the pace was proving difficult but eventually our trainee began to accelerate. Quite soon she was making us run. At this rate and, worryingly, we wouldn't be able to keep up.

Blood pumping in my head seemed to coincide with feet pounding on the road. Maybe I was having a heart attack. What a way to go.

'Look up!' I cried. Margaret seemed to be

hypnotised by the pedals but managed to lift her head.

'No, not the sky, you daftie. Ahead!'

And then, with a burst of speed to leave us standing, she was off! Freed from restraint she was launched. Helpless we watched. The large blob that was Margaret grew smaller by the minute. She was making a zig-zag course towards the perils of Grosvenor Road where the sound of her wails slowly faded into the distance.

19

DRIVING WITH CARE

Marie had given herself up to disaster, burying her face in her hands and moaning. 'She's heading for traffic – she's going to be killed. Oh why did we ever think we could help? We'll be in such trouble. Mother of God! I knew I should have stayed with my geriatrics back home.'

'Shush a moment, Marie.' I'd been diverted by something quite extraordinary. 'Hang on a sec. Look, it must be Cinderella time. There's a pumpkin on the loose.' Marie spread her fingers to look through them. 'Sure pumpkins don't move,' she whispered.

'Well then it must be Cynthia. See that gold shape lurking in the bushes? Open your eyes, see? It looks as if she needs to get away but she's not sure where. She's weaving about like she's lost, and oh, Lord.' Small whimpering sounds floated towards us. 'I think she must be crying.'

Marie shook her head in disbelief then, taking in the agitated figure, registered with a start. As quickly forgetting her pledge to care only for the elderly, she snapped into Sister Mercy mode and said, 'Ah – the wee love! Look, you're good at running. You go after Margaret and I'll see to Cynthia. Sure but she sounds really upset – the poor soul. What could've gone wrong?'

'I dunno but actually, and if I know her, the last thing she'll want is us fussing over her. This must be one of the few occasions Cynthia doesn't need an audience.' I peered into the dark but saw nothing until nose blowing tones trumpeted from behind a bush marked her position. 'I think we should leave her for the moment, track down Evel Knievel and see if there're any bits left. I wouldn't mind hearing tears coming from that direction. At least we'd know she's alive. Come on, let's hurry. We can come back and check on Cynthia once we've found Margaret.'

In worrying mode, we started to jog along the seemingly endless stretch to Grosvenor

Road. 'At least we're on the right track, see. Look,' Marie said, pointing to a swathe cut through a flower bed, 'I never noticed them before.'

'Well let's hope nobody else sees them either or they'll be on the hunt for a phantom pruner and,' I was beginning to struggle, 'maybe we shouldn't mention Cynthia to Margaret when and if we find her. Where on earth do you think she is?'

And still there was no sightings. I looked back but there was neither sight nor sound. Cynthia had disappeared completely. Presumably she'd got back into the hospital by the District entrance. I hoped she was all right. The idea of her being anything other than in charge, even if it was just of herself, was unimaginable. And where was Dr Welch in her hour of need?

We'd reached Grosvenor Road and, scanning it, at last saw with a surge of relief, Margaret with the bike – both apparently in one piece.

'Praise be! But she's talking to a bobby,' whispered Marie, clutching my shoulder. 'I hope she hasn't been arrested.'

'From the way they're talking I don't think that's what he's got in mind. He seems to be showing her how the bike lights work. Come on, let's say hello and find out.'

Despite the odds, Margaret appeared hale and hearty and in remarkably good spirits.

'Hello there, girls. Did you think you'd lost me?' If it had been anybody but Margaret I'd have sworn she sounded roguish.

'Would these be the two you were telling me about?' The policeman was big and cheerful with the easy manner of somebody practised in crowd control. 'Yez have chosen a quair time to be out on a cycling mission surely?' He put his hand on the handlebars as if we might grab the bike and escape. 'I'm thinking this young lady,' he nodded at Margaret, 'has been in dangerous company.'

'As on the bike?' I said, liking him for the fun in his voice, the absence of a notebook, the way he'd obviously helped Margaret but wasn't making a meal of it and the fact that he was bigger than her.

'That too.'

'Brian's been telling me I should've had my lights on,' Margaret explained, 'and I've been telling him I'm just a learner. I nearly ran him down you know.'

'We police don't often get a chance to stop women on runaway bikes but maybe you should think about getting some more practice.' Brian was all but pulling on his braces. 'If you like, I could help. I've had a fair bit of experience and I'd hate some poor woman in labour waiting for her midwife to call and her never arriving on account of her transport letting her down.'

Marie seemed to have been struck dumb

by Brian's magisterial presence but now she managed, 'Is that not a great offer, Margaret, and maybe the sergeant here can take you and the bike back, even help you have another wee shot? Jane and I won't mind. It would let us take the long way round to the Home.' A gust of wind with a suggestion of hail whipped her hair, tilting her halo. 'Sure and it's a fine night for a breath of fresh air.'

Margaret was enthusiastic. 'Good idea.' She waved a dismissive gauntlet. 'I'm so excited. I can't believe I've learnt so quickly. Now I just want to get better and,' her nostrils flared, 'I'm sure I can trust Brian not to let me go.'

The policeman placed a territorial hand on the bike seat. 'And I won't be doing that. Dedicated midwives are thin on the ground. I should know. My late mother was one. She'd have been delighted to think I was helping you to become one. So just you hop on the saddle, Margaret. And it's hi-ho, Silver and cheerio, girls.'

We could have said, 'Mind how you go', but they were already gone, Brian striding alongside Margaret who might have been wobbling but in all other respects was in complete control.

'Wait till she starts telling him about theatre,' I said.

'But at least she's happy and safe,' sighed Marie, tucking her arm into mine. 'I wish

190

we could say the same for Cynthia. When we get back I'm wondering if we'll see her. See if she's all right. I'll be praying for her if not.'

'Marie, do you ever think about yourself?'

She looked puzzled. 'Of course I do. All the time. How else could I be of service to others and,' she paused as if holding the winning card, 'it's what helps me get out of bed in the morning.'

In the end, and despite heavy lurking outside Cynthia's bedroom, we'd to wait until morning when a bleary-eyed Seonaid, granting us an audience in her bedroom, gave us some answers.

20

A LECTURE FROM CYNTHIA

'We're just checking you'd a good time,' Marie said, stepping cautiously into the room where Seonaid's hairpiece nestled like a small rodent on top of her dress, which had been flung on the floor.

'They look as if they'd a good time and must have danced all night,' I offered, picking up battle-scarred shoes placed neatly by her bed and tapping the soles together. 'Morning, campers!'

Seonaid sat up in her bed and held a hand over her eye. 'Would you stop that racket and take that rat-tat-tat out of my ear? I can't believe you're waking me on a day off. Me head's bursting now.'

I gave up on the subtle approach. 'And so's ours – with curiosity. How did last night go? You must've been late. I never heard you coming in.'

'Nor I,' agreed Marie. 'You must've been having a great time. I was thinking about you all night and still I never heard you.'

'It was OK,' Seonaid shrugged. 'I've been at worse.'

'Is that a love bite on your neck?' I asked, making Seonaid get up and rush over to the mirror. 'Caught you! If there hadn't been a chance of one you'd never have gone to check.'

She had the grace to laugh. 'I suppose Raymond did his best to give me a good time and the tickets were expensive.' A belated sigh of conscience seemed to engulf her before she went on, 'And the food was great, even if we were sitting below Cynthia's lot.'

I said, 'Now! Cynthia? Marie and I heard her last night when we were out with Margaret. She was roaming outside, round the bushes and sounded really upset. She was home even before we were. We saw the light in her room but didn't want to disturb her, and she's out this morning. Miss Mac-

192

Cready said she'd seen her heading off very early on. D'you know what happened?'

Seonaid lay back on her bed, putting her head on the pillows as if it were a treasured possession and sighed. 'That oulde yoke Welch acted as if he wasn't with her. It was a shame. He just went off and danced with other girls. You'd have thought he was on his own. Cynthia did as best she could, but eventually being left in a corner got too much for her and she left.' Seonaid shook her head. 'I didn't know if she'd have liked me to do anything but I thought it might hurt her pride if I did. I asked Raymond to have a word with her supposed partner but he was already having several with that obstetrician, Jimmy, who took exception to him asking Lisa to dance. How did you know about Cynthia?'

I told her about our own adventures. She seemed to think they were as exciting as the Ball and, as full of curiosity about Margaret as we'd been about Cynthia, wondered if she'd got home alright.

I said, 'Yes. I was up early but not as early as her. She was in the dining room having breakfast and looking like the cat who's eaten the cream. She couldn't wait to tell me she's meeting Brian later on.' I jogged Seonaid's arm. 'Believe it or not, she's got a date!'

'Well, so have I,' said Seonaid, yawning, 'and it's with my bed. I might not sleep worrying about her, so go and see if you can find Cynthia.'

'Why do we get all the good jobs?' I asked, unsure if a missing Cynthia was cause for alarm. 'She'll probably bite our heads off if we do run into her.'

'I've to go to Mass first but that won't take long. If you like, you could even come with me. I'm sure you'd like it.' Marie's eyes shone. A conversion might just be within her grasp.

'No thanks. You go to church and I'll go and see if I can run into her but she could be anywhere. Maybe I should try the graveyard. I sometimes go there for a think, myself.'

'You never!' Marie was startled. 'Holy Mother, but you're full of surprises. Are you not frightened of ghosts? There's bound to be loads there.'

'I haven't met any as yet. It's usually nice and quiet, but if I do, I'll take one home to you even if you've got your own Holy One waiting for you. Come on, you'll miss Mass if you don't go now.' I ushered Marie out the door, then, pausing before following, asked, 'Um – Seonaid – was Oliver there?'

She opened one eye, 'No. Bridie, his ex-girlfriend was. Partnering one of the other students in their crowd.' She snuggled down before adding, 'Raymond says she and Oliver have settled on being just good friends. Interested?'

'No. Curious,' I said as firmly as I shut the door.

Pursuing the matter of Cynthia, I asked Miss MacCready if she'd seen her.

'No – but I wasn't looking for her.' She gave a dismissive jangle of her bracelet. 'Sure she's a big girl. Should be able to fend for herself, but what about you? Where in all the wide world are you off to?'

It sounded as if she might have been choked off by Cynthia, who must be returning to form. I gave up worrying about her.

'It looks like a nice day. I think I'll go for a wee walk to get some fresh air.' I was aware that if I as much as mentioned a cemetery, the receptionist, in her kindly way, would engage delaying tactics until she contacted The Samaritans.

I liked the Falls Road graveyard. It had the same melancholy charm as the one off Aberdeen's Union Street where the sound of traffic was hushed by ancient walls, and benches on well-ordered paths offered resting places for the undead.

It was a perfect spot to cast aside the determinedly cheerful front prescribed for the caring profession. There were sad epitaphs on the graves which bore witness to those who hadn't survived any kind of medicine. If it wasn't for the sound of a gravedigger leisurely working to the sound of 'Music While You Work' I reckoned I could get a good gloom going here.

I found a spot as far away from the tinny tranny's sound as possible and sat opposite a stone angel curiously resembling Queen Victoria. This one stretched forward, hand extended, as if thumbing a lift from her bus shelter-like arbour. There was ivy everywhere but it was particularly rampant over a nearby group of unmarked graves. They recorded the lot of paupers and children, fallen victims to the infectious diseases now eliminated by modern medicine.

I'd a lump in my throat as I considered a gravestone marking the death of eight children. There were many others who'd died and they hadn't even their burial places marked. As if in mourning, the bare trees heaved and groaned, their dead leaves collected into darkly-sodden heaps. The Black Mountain, chief of the surrounding hills, looked down, bleak and uncaring. Any moment now there was going to be a cloudburst. Cautiously, I looked around hoping the gravedigger wouldn't think consoling a girl in tears was part of his job.

This was a strange land where religious beliefs competed, bringing tension, judgement and, as far as I could see, unhappiness. My old training school was held in poor regard and here the Midwifery training was full of sweat, tears and a labour not confined to the patients to whom our responsibilities stretched unendingly. It only needed the addition of an unasked-for kiss in a sluice – a sluice! Then a dash of homesickness, and any minute now I'd get a good bawl going.

I got my hanky out in preparation, drew breath and was just about to let go, when a couple in black approached. Flowers in hand they looked full of grief and as if they were coming to tend the fresh grave opposite.

Plainly it wasn't the time for self-pity. I rose and, donning a suitably reverent expression, moved quickly away, eyes humbly to the ground. Minutes later I banged straight into a happier couple – Margaret and Brian.

A graveyard seemed an unlikely setting but they both seemed as cheerful as if they were on a relaxed day's outing. Even Margaret's lipstick was bang on target.

Brian, particularly informal in an open shirt, tweed jacket and flannels said, 'We do meet in strange places. We're just visiting my mother's grave before Margaret and I have a cycle test drive. I'm hoping we'll have a wee tour.' His smile was easy as he put his arm round Margaret's waist. 'She's a quick learner.'

Margaret blushed. 'And what would you be doing here, Jane?'

I didn't think they would understand that the Scots psyche could be recharged by gloom so I vaguely hinted at an interest in

local history. It could be useful for the background research we were bound to need at
some point in our training.

Margaret stuck out her chin as she re-
secured her headsquare so tightly it looked
as if she wanted to shut out sound. 'You're
too conscientious,' she said, linking her arm
firmly through Brian's. 'It's a day off, for
heaven's sake. Anyway, you sound as if
you've a cold coming on. Why don't you
head back to the Home and have a hot drink
and an aspirin? You want to be well for
working in the nursery and not snivelling all
over the babies, don't you?'

She should have been more concerned
about my bunion. A day later, my inherit-
ance from winkle-picker days was throbbing
in the compulsory overshoes needed for
working in the Special Care Nursery. In a
unit where humidity would be useful for preparing for life in the tropics, my throbbing
foot was making its own thermal contri-
bution. It was as well for me we did most of
our work sitting down.

Although it was gratifying getting a small
movement from a tiny limb in answer to a
gentle stroke, other than feeding, fretting
over and checking conversationally-limited
babies, there wasn't much else to do. The
resident staff were so experienced they
appeared to work on automatic pilot so that

tube and bottle feeding were carried out with the smooth efficiency of a bottling factory. What with the stifling atmosphere and my bunion shooting hot needles of pain, I even began to look forward to the weekly lecture slot.

'Are you limping?' asked Seonaid, taking an arm as we headed into the lecture hall. 'You're like an oulde woman there. You'd best sit at the front and save a bit of travel time.'

'I don't want to do that. I'll be right under Prof. McQuaid's eye,' I complained, but Seonaid and her micro-second sympathy had gone.

Margaret had moved with her. The change of her circumstances had put paid to the glorious fields of study and endeavour she had so actively promoted when we'd first arrived. All she could talk about now was a policeman's lot, the joys of exercise and life in the saddle.

'Ah! Jane!' Cynthia plumped down beside me. 'I see Margaret's taking a back seat. Well, at least you'll make a change from her endless talk about that policeman chap she's taken up with. Honestly, she's becoming such a drag.'

'Not as boring as the Prof., I bet. Look, here he comes with Miss Harvey. She looks a bit fussed. I suppose she's on edge after the spat with him about our class and the witnessing deliveries saga.'

Plainly Cynthia wanted to be reminded of this as little as of the Medic's Ball, after which she had reappeared somewhat crushed and a lot quieter. I hadn't the heart to ask her about it, especially as she was spinning a silly 'walking into a door' yarn explaining Dr Welch's black eye.

Apparently, Dr O'Reilly, tiring of the house doctor's fixation with his partner, Lisa, had administered a rough justice. I thought it magnificent if unprofessional.

It was unimaginable that the Professor was ever in a similar situation or was even a dancer. Certainly not wearing that green Donegal tweed suit, today's sartorial outfit. He'd have melted on the spot.

He bounced into the lecture hall in the manner of someone accustomed to respectful attention and, throwing his raincoat over a chair, checked his sparse grey hair still lay dutifully across his shiny dome. He looked upon his audience with the disfavour of someone who'd stepped on something nasty.

'Yes, yes, I know this class,' he said, interrupting Miss Harvey's surprisingly timid introduction. 'Strangers to the truth. Well, let's see if they can cope with real facts. Where's the head and pelvis?'

It wasn't much of an audience warm-up and it wasn't going to get any better. As the

Professor began his lecture, machine-gun rattling out the facts from a small trap of a mouth, he whisked the doll's head to and fro through the pelvis so fast it became a blur and my mind wandered off. I wondered if it was true he was an examiner for our First Part Midwifery exam. If he was, then, judging by the stultifying atmosphere of his lecture, I didn't much fancy our success rates.

Still he droned on. I was too frightened to yawn but Cynthia didn't have that problem. Apparently the Medical Ball experience hadn't left her entirely chastened as she folded her arms, sighed, fidgeted, examined her fingernails and stretched her legs as if to stop blood clots forming. Under her wearied gaze our lecturer was beginning to falter. I too had begun to squirm, but that was with pain. I'd really need to do something about this foot.

Suddenly the Professor narrowed his eyes, went an unbecoming pink then shouted, 'Right!' He was looking straight at Cynthia. In an exasperated gesture he lobbed both doll's head and pelvis at her, 'I don't think any of you have been listening to a word I've been saying. You, girl, repeat what I've just been saying.'

I ducked, relieved mightily when, with the careless ease of a tennis player, Cynthia reached out and caught both objects. In a leisurely way she stood up then, holding them like objets d'art, she moved to the front to face the class.

'Perhaps it's best I sit, then you'll all see better and you, Professor, might like to take a seat with the rest of the class. Oh thank you, Miss Harvey, but don't you want your seat?'

'No thanks, I'll go and sit at the back. I'll get a really good view there.' Miss Harvey sounded amused whilst the Professor, looking surprised, took Cynthia's place, frowning whilst she calmly laid the head and pelvis on her estuary of a lap.

'Understanding the mechanism of labour is relatively easy,' she began. 'It just takes a little application coupled with simplicity of expression.' She cleared her throat, then in a precise but lucid way she repeated the Professor's lecture, only this time she had everybody's attention.

We craned forward, hanging on her every word. Cynthia was making this a lot clearer – even fun. The doll's head looked as if it had more life in it than some of my Nursery tinies as, responding to its puppet master's hands, it cheerily popped through the positions the Professor had made so sleep-inducing. Even the pelvis with its bony structure seemed polished and keen to star.

'And that of course as we all know is the very best position for the baby's head before delivery,' said Cynthia as she finished. 'See? Left occipito anterior – or as we would probably say, L.O.A.' She swept the doll's head through the pelvis with a flourish and stood up. 'And it's what we all want as caring professionals,' she said, looking straight at the Professor, 'for our patients. Now has anybody any questions?'

Miss Harvey, looking pleased, came to the front putting her hands together as if in applause and at last awarding Cynthia her full title. 'I must say, I think Nurse Brown-Smythe has done a good summing-up job. Maybe she could become our next lecturer. That would certainly free your *valuable* time up wouldn't it, Professor?'

The Professor took off his spectacles, breathed on them, cleaned them, replaced them then, clearing his throat, stood up.

'Well, she's certainly covered most points,' he said grudgingly. 'I just hope everybody was listening.' He was obviously still nursing a vendetta and, deprived of a victim, he looked round, letting his gaze fall on me. 'So maybe we should put it to the test again.' Behind the rimless specs, his eyes gleamed as if they too had been polished. 'You'll have no excuse for getting the mechanism of labour wrong now, so why not give us another quick run-through?'

My heart sank. Nobody could repeat Cynthia's slick performance. Anyway, my brain had relocated to my foot where there was far more activity. Flustered, I stood up. Then did what only could be done under such a trial of strength – fainted.

21

CARE ON THE HOME FRONT

When I came to, I was being wheeled along the corridor in a chair helmed by Miss Harvey and pushed by Seonaid. Unsure if my grogginess was due to the relief of a rapid exit or the pain from a very angry foot, I discovered we were heading for the staff sick bay. Recovery became an imperative.

Fully conscious now I said, 'I'm fine – just a little light-headed. I skipped breakfast – honestly.'

'Rubbish!' Miss Harvey fingered her pelican badge. The gleaming emblem under her collar was a hard-won symbol of excellence from an Edinburgh training school. The badge showed a bird feeding its young. Known to do so from their own blood, the badge illustrated an act representing charity and self-sacrifice.

Miss Harvey had apparently found an authoritative, no-nonsense approach as effective. 'By the look of that toe joint, you've got gout and the best cure for that is bed, so let's get you into one.'

She was leading at such a brisk pace Seonaid's feet were moving into a speed I'd have loved to have managed.

'Gout!' Surely that was the fate of choleric-hued colonels paying for a life of excess. 'What a humiliation.'

'Nurse Brown-Smythe's phoned Ward Sister to let her know you're coming.' Plainly, Cynthia was still in Miss Harvey's favour.

Gloom descended. We were all now going to have to cope with the prospect of Cynthia's new status as 'person in charge'. Doubtless she'd have diagnosed the bunion. I bet she'd wrenched off the shoe which now lay in my lap. Maybe I should be grateful I hadn't had a heart attack. I wouldn't put it past Cynthia to go for glory in open-heart surgery. Still, she hadn't put out the Belisha beacon flashing at the end of my leg.

'Mother of God but it's hard keeping up with that woman,' muttered Seonaid, breaking into a trot. 'So where have you been doing this high living?'

'All along the Falls, of course. I just wish I was there instead of here, and at the rate we're going I'll be lucky to arrive in one bit. Mind that corner! I'm going to tell Raymond you're an even worse driver than he is.'

'Ah, sure, and I could give him a lesson or two. Look we're nearly there.' We'd left the maternity hospital and arrived at a small outbuilding. It was tucked behind the District block, probably strategically hidden since a designated place for sick members of staff mightn't be the best advertisement for hospital care.

Marie was hovering outside. 'You'll be needing this.' Her eyes brimmed concern as she handed over a bag of belongings out of which stuck a Bible. Putting her hand to her mouth, and well out of Miss Harvey's ear-shot, she whispered, 'I've only packed the essentials. I'll take other things to you later. Now would you like me to phone your parents?'

'No thanks. I'm going to be fine. I'll be back with you in no time.'

'I wouldn't be too sure of that.' A small, brisk Sister in a pristinely white coat had appeared. Her name tag said she was Sister Ann, which might have intended inform-ality, except that from her cap to her white shoes, she was squeaky clean.

'Come away!' It was like being addressed by a scrubbed-up surgeon.

She grimaced as Seonaid, bumping me up the steps, aimed for the door. In a proprie-tary way, she grabbed the wheelchair. 'Here, let me take that chair before you make my patient a road traffic accident. Then she might have to go to the big boys in Casualty and, Miss Harvey, I expect you need to get back to your class even though your colleague on the phone said not to hurry. Who was that, by the way? I didn't recognise the voice but she sounded very confident.'

'Oh she's that alright,' Miss Harvey sighed, 'but she's *only* a student, like these two. Anyway, we'd better get back before I lose my job.'

'Sounds a nightmare,' murmured Sister, now bowling me along a corridor off which were side rooms where, presumably, staff members were kept in splendid isolation – or perhaps splendid staff members had privacy.

'So you trained in Aberdeen then?'

I nodded, expecting the usual response but got a break.

'That's where the typhoid was,' she mused. 'Read all about it in the paper. People dying all over the place.'

I was too busy clinging on to protest it wasn't the case. Aberdeen's medical staff had dealt well with their patients who'd all recovered from what was an acutely infectious disease. But Sister Ann was concentrating all her energy on whisking her fare into a small surgery with shelves full of bottles filled with brightly-coloured lotions.

'You'll know about barrier nursing I suppose? Handy knowledge to have for keeping down infection so,' she clicked her teeth thoughtfully, 'just in case there's more to that bunion than meets the eye, we'll just confine you to your room.' She donned a mask then, swivelling on her heel, ran busy little fingers over the bottles, as if about to make a spell. 'So there'll be no roaming about.'

She waved a cautionary finger. 'Now let's see what we can do here. Ha! This looks good.' She picked up a small stainless-steel bowl then poured from a bottle marked 'Red Lotion' some liquid, its colour even brighter than my bunion which was by now radiating heat waves.

She shook a white swab from a packet into the pot and watched as it turned pink. 'Ah! Soaking nicely! Now, stick out that leg and we'll put this on that red light area and see what happens.' She fished the swab out with forceps then brushed it over my foot with artistic dexterity.

The 'Red Lotion' had an immediate effect. The infection in my toe joint tried to fight back, but succumbing to the liquid's soothing quality, settled for a gentle throb. There was just enough power left to register its presence. Already and miraculously my big toe, its swollen joint throwing it off course, began to consider realigning itself with its companions.

I eyed Sister Ann with great respect. 'It

feels better already. That's good stuff you've got there. Maybe I should drink it as well.'

'Better not – it's got arsenic in it. Now let's get you into bed and we'll get your temperature taken. You look a bit flushed to me.'

That was the trouble with nurses looking after nurses, I mused as I was tipped into bed – you couldn't be sure when they were joking. On the one hand, I'd been made to feel better but, on the other, worse because of the arsenic and the typhoid remark. Still, if it meant I'd have a nice bright room, then even if the bedclothes had a thing like a rat cage taking their weight, it wasn't all bad news. It might be a bit chilly about the feet but maybe the draught would lower my temperature and lying down was infinitely preferable to a stumble through the mechanism of labour.

Sister Ann advanced with a form and a thermometer, the latter of which she stuck in my mouth.

'I've got most of your details, but I don't seem to have your religion.'

'Hmm, arrgh.'

'Really? I'm a minister's wife myself. Good to see the faith being kept in far-flung shores.' You'd have thought she was referring to the mission fields.

She tapped her teeth with her biro. 'And nice that you're not with that Paisley lot and their preaching hatred. And sure, they'd take money off a beggar so they would.'

I tried to tell her I wasn't anything, but by the time she took off her mask and removed the thermometer, it was too late. The form had disappeared and she had the look of someone with other pressing matters. She cleared her throat and leant forward, looking so serious I wondered if she was going to admit she was a closet Catholic or I was due an amputation.

'Haggis.'

'Haggis?'

She blushed, concentrating on a finger straightening the counterpane. 'Is it true you can only get them in Scotland?'

I chuckled. After her crack about typhoid Sister Ann deserved a leg pull. 'Yes. We're very proud of our natural species.'

'And they can only go round hills?'

'Definitely, it's the two left legs shorter than the front ones that does it. Heaven knows how they ever get caught as they only go out at night.'

She was enthralled. 'I've seen pictures of haggis, but they look kind of bald.'

I was beginning to enjoy myself. 'That's because they lose their hair in the chase. It's the fright that does it.'

'Well I wouldn't be wanting to meet one out in the dark. Would they bite?'

'Only if you shine a torch on them.'

'There'd be no danger of that.' She spoke

sharply as if already practising how she'd handle peril. 'Anyway, I'm never going to Scotland. Now why don't you get some sleep?'

I must have taken Sister Ann's advice. When I awoke it was dark. There were no lights anywhere. I must have slept for ever. Certain proof of a life threatening illness? A now-diminished foot throb from the bottom of the bed might have suggested I was returning to health, but then I heard whispers surrounding the bed. Hallucinations surely.

Then, accompanied by a sharp poke, came the smell of fish and chips and Seonaid's very real voice. 'Are ye awake there? Look, we've brought you some tayties.' She banged on the light.

'Oh turn it off!' Like a child making itself invisible, Marie threw her hands over her eyes. 'We're not supposed to be here. We'll get in awful trouble if anyone finds us. It's so late and all.'

'Nobody's minding the place. We sailed in, cool as a breeze, and sure, Jane's not that important,' Seonaid said, rustling in the chip bag. 'Here, have one.' She was wearing a hat knitted for her by a grateful patient who'd used extra wool to add on long lugs. They made her look as if she'd pigtails.

Eyeing the rapidly-diminishing pile of chips I took one and waved it in the direction of my feet. 'This is for you, Little Pigs.'

'I don't think wee piggies like chips,' said Marie doubtfully.

'Well some do,' I said, eyeing Seonaid.

'I'd say she's more like a milkmaid?' Marie meant it kindly, watching Seonaid pulling on her plaits as if tugging teats, 'but we need to be heading off now. We only came to see you're alright.' Already she was heading for the door.

'And at least we've established you are, with appetite fully recovered,' Seonaid observed, savouring the last chip. And even cheeky about pigs and OK, Marie, maybe we should be going. We'll tell the others you're definitely on the mend and likely to be back on duty soon.' She tapped my foot lightly.

Pleased that it didn't scream I said, 'Sister Ann's done a wonderful job but I'm not that keen to go back to the hothouse. It didn't do my bunion any good.'

'Ah, but you're not going back to the Nursery. We're all going on night duty. You'll be in Pussy MacNutt's ward. She's a doll but whatever you do, don't cross Sally.'

'Sally?'

'She's the ward maid. Sour! Drives a trolley like a tank. You need to watch she doesn't run over that foot of yours.'

'And Pussy?'

'Ah, sure and you'll find out soon enough,' said Seonaid, and then they were gone,

Marie's squeaks and Seonaid's pattering footstep fading into the distance like the sound of mice behind the wainscot.

Sister Ann came in the following day, made straight for my foot, looked at it then, seeming pleased, said, 'Well now, Nurse Macpherson, that's looking better, another couple of days bed rest and you'll be back to pounding the wards – good as new.'

'Um, Sister – about haggis...'

22

POST-NATAL BLUES

When I'd made that visit to Denise in the post-natal ward Sister MacNutt must have been off duty. She'd have been hard to miss, being very tall, wearing huge white shoes and the letterbox-red Sister's uniform. Her arms were so long she could easily handle a dozen babies in one go.

With a recent experience making feet of special interest, I found Pussy's particularly fascinating. They were huge. Not only did they help her cover the ground fast but they were surprisingly soft-footed. They earned her the Pussy title even if cats don't wear bifocal specs.

Along with Mrs Blair, my auxiliary partner for the night, we waited in the corridor
outside Pussy's office. Suddenly, as if out of
nowhere, she was there.

She glanced over the top of her glasses
then down at a baby swinging in the crook of
her arm. 'And see, Little Connor, if it's not
night staff! Is it that time already? We'll just
give you to your mother, shall we? Goodness
knows, she needs the practice.' She disappeared into Denise's old room where her
soothing tones had an instant effect on a dis-
gruntled patient. The baby, less impressed,
started wailing.

Mrs Blair had the hardened expression of
an experienced night worker faced with a
rookie. After tonight, she'd be due time off
so she wouldn't have very long to knock this
one into shape. Knitting needles sticking
out of her bag suggested multi-tasking but
hopefully not including cattle prodding.

'By the time that woman's ready to be a
mammy, her baby'll be ready for school.'
Mrs Blair cast her eyes heavenward. 'It's a
good thing she's in a room on her own, she's
so anxious with that baby she'd put the
other mothers in the same state as herself.'
Her rosebud mouth tightened.

'So what about that racket?' I asked, pointing to a nearby door, behind which noise of
crockery came crashing as if thrown from a

distance, 'That's not very reassuring for anybody. It sounds as if somebody's going into battle.'

'Ach, they're used to that one alright. It's only Sally with the night-time drinks. Mind out! Here she comes.'

A ward maid, grim in intent and purpose, flung the door open and approached with a trolley. Now, picking up speed, surging forward and firing on all cylinders she passed us, looking straight ahead with the concentration of a night train driver. In her wake, a smell of bleach hung as unpleasantly as that of exhaust fumes.

Impressed at how nimbly the middle-aged Mrs Blair had leapt to safety, I'd followed to watch. The drinks trolley, chattering like a noisy meeting, reached a crescendo whilst driven through the main ward's swing doors as if they didn't exist.

'Tay, Missus?'

'You'll have heard Sally?' asked Pussy with a faint smile. Without the baby, her arms dangled like badly-hung washing until she tucked them in tidy loops under her armpits. 'She likes to get the drinks out and in before she goes off duty. She's very particular about her kitchen. Doesn't really like anybody else in it. And of course Matron's very strict about that sort of thing too.' She unfurled an arm to let it wander octopus-like to scratch her nose. 'No patients allowed, of course.

Hygiene's so important, though I don't suppose I need to tell you that.'

'Sally'll just have to suffer me,' Mrs Blair sniffed. 'How does she think I can get the water to heat up the babbies' bottles?' She nodded into the nursery where three babies lay in cots numbered rather than named. 'And I suppose I'll be the one feeding these.'

I was curious about this trio. They lay so still I hoped they were alright and, since they were the only ones there, wondered why they weren't with their mothers. Mrs Blair continued, 'Oh well I suppose The Illigits will be leaving soon.' Which, even if it was an unfortunate way of putting it, saved me asking.

Pussy grimaced as if somebody had trodden on her tail then gave a gentle sigh. 'We'll need to remember: it's not their fault and they're certainly no bother. I haven't heard a squeak from any of them all day. But maybe you should make a start on feeding them now, Mrs Blair.'

Mrs Blair, looking righteous, turned her wedding ring like it was a badge of honour then sped off, declaring the babies were going to be better off than many as they were going to decent homes and to people who could provide for them.

I followed Pussy into her office. The cross-stitch texts framed on the walls suggested a simple outlook, but the picture of a thatched cottage surely wasn't her home – she'd never have fitted into it.

She folded herself behind a tidy desk and flicked rapidly through the Kardex report on the patients. It was obvious that care in a postnatal ward, even if equally good, was a far cry from the more urgent demands of a general hospital.

'It's important the mothers get an undisturbed sleep,' said Pussy. 'So all the babies are taken into the Nursery at night.' She waved a warning finger. 'But no playing with them, mind. Just feed them if they cry. We want them going home conditioned to sleep at night. We don't wake the breast-feeding mums either – they'll get plenty sleepless nights when they get home.'

I reckoned Mrs Blair, with her practical air, would be fully occupied with her knitting whilst I'd never thought playing with babies was a midnight pastime. However, I did wonder about the numbered babies. Day staff would be too busy to give them any special attention. Deprived of maternal loving care, where would they get it?

Other than an awareness that unmarried mothers were considered the lowest of the low I couldn't remember anything in the textbooks dealing with them and their babies.

'Do the unmarried mothers get to nurse their babies?' I asked.

A pause then a suggestion of claw. 'No!'

Obviously, when it came to babies born out of wedlock the Swinging Sixties had by-passed Belfast, yet Pussy seemed uncomfortable with the question.

'As soon as they have their six days here and are all right, they'll be discharged, probably to homes for unmarried mothers.' Her shoulders slumped. 'It's hard for them – but what's their choice? Anyway, none of these girls have asked to see their babies, so it's probably best for everybody that they get on with their lives. At least they'll know their babies are going to caring homes.'

'What's your opinion of the way they deal with unmarried mothers?' I asked, spirits lightened a little by Lorna's easy way and ready smile. She was sharing a space in the restaurant with a textbook whilst macaroni and cheese lay congealing beside her.

A night duty meal here was a subdued affair. The water feature had been switched off, the lights dimmed and there was no Belfast Daisy to bossily brighten up the self-service counter. What night staff there was talked in hunched groups lost in the huge room.

Had it not been for Sally's moratoria on her kitchen I'd have been tempted to make a sandwich there instead. Maybe Mrs Blair, who was knitting an Aran sweater, would have shown me how. I was as impressed by her ability to follow a complicated pattern blind as by her expert handling of the babies.

'Ah sure, you'll get good at handling babies too,' she said with the irritatingly confident way of a professional who knows there's no danger of challenge.

In her care, all but the trio gurgled and cooed whilst her fingers, knitting-nimble, sorted and changed them. She bottle-fed hungry mouths with the careless efficiency of a petrol pump attendant. I wouldn't have been surprised if she'd whipped open her uniform and provided some home brew to the breastfed babies herself.

'Feckin' brutal!' Lorna's response to the question of unmarried mothers was immediate. She slammed the book shut and picked up a fork. 'It's enough to put you off being a midwife. The trouble, of course, is that pregnancy outside marriage is considered a mortal sin.' She sliced the air with her fork. 'Shameful! I believe some poor girls even come up from the country to have their babies here so that their family'll never know. Then they go home, lightened of baby and burdened by a secret instead.'

'Maybe that's why my ones keep themselves to themselves. I've tried talking to them but they don't respond. They're a bit like their babies, locked away in their own wee world. They even seem to want screens pulled round their beds all the time.' Thinking of such shuttered withdrawals made me uneasy.

'Sounds as if post-natal's hardly a breeze then?'

'No! And it's not helped by the fact that I've got to give a baby-bathing demo in the morning. Pussy seemed to think I could do with a diversion and there's a dopey mother needing some intensive mothercare lessons. Pussy reckoned it'll be good practice but I'm not sure for who.'

Lorna gave her endearing chuckle. 'It's the great unknown, isn't it? I've just had to learn how to release a mother from the safety pins holding her underwear together. It didn't help that she came in at the height of labour. Speak about getting out of a tight spot!'

She was obviously trying to cheer me up. In the same way the next morning I was trying to get Mrs O'Shea to spring out of bed and greet the day with a loud 'Hurrah!'

'Try it with s-stitches.' Her face was pale, her eyes huge and she was so big I just hoped there weren't any more babies left inside. With trembling hands she fumbled with a bed jacket straining at the button-holes then, blowing a strand of hair to clear her vision, she struggled out onto a chair. Despite a rubber ring strategically placed, she sat on it as if sitting on a gorse bush.

'Jasus! And I'm expected to hold a baby – never mind bathe him.'

'Everybody's nervous to begin with. Best feed him first.' I was hearty. 'Believe you me, you'll soon get the hang of Connor.'

But word must have got out in the nursery, and Connor had already consulted his book of rights. With little waving fists and a bright red face he was registering anxiety in loud yells. Mrs O'Shea looked on in such a fearful way you'd have thought I was Herod hunting the newborn.

'Ach, he's just a hungry wee bairnie,' I said, stoppering Connor and his yells with a bottle and putting him into his mother's arms. 'Look at that now!'

'Ah! You wee dote!' Even though she held the bottle like a dart, Connor was happy. There was no way he was going to let go of that bottle and this seemed to give Mrs O'Shea confidence. She jigged him a bit then, stopping to allow him a very satisfactory burp, managed to pat his bald head. 'You sound and look just like your daddy.'

Pleased with progress so far I told her we'd graduate to a bathing demonstration. 'We'll have that bairn bathed before he knows he's in the water.' In full tutorial mode I rolled up my sleeves and filled a basin.

Mrs O'Shea clutched Connor to her. 'But what about his cork?'

'Huh?'

She pointed.

It was time to get technical,

'You mean his belly button?'

Outside, a new day was arriving, whilst inside came the sound of crockery crashes. Sally must be back and in her fiefdom.

Blast! She was early and bound to have found one of the single girls in there. Earlier on, I'd happened on Maureen in the toilet where she was trying to muffle tears so heart rending she was incapable of speech.

It was such difficult territory I didn't know what to do or say. One thing Belfast seemed to share with Aberdeen was that feelings were considered best kept secret and patients kept out of the kitchens.

I'd cursed the customs, patted her on the shoulder and offered a tissue. Aware she wanted her grief kept private, I'd suggested the kitchen as a bolthole. It might be Sally's patch but I was willing to live dangerously. Anyway, she wouldn't be on duty for ages.

'And whilst you're there, make yourself a cup of tea. It's nice and quiet and at least you'll get some privacy. Stay as long as you like. Just don't let Sally or, worse, Matron catch you.'

In her brisk way Mrs Blair was getting the babies to their mothers for their morning feed. She was fully occupied and so, caught up with a new baby and mother, was I, until now.

I glanced at Connor. Exhaustion had caught up with him. Having struck for the far shores of the baby bath, been lassoed by a towel, dried and finally dredged in a snow flurry of talcum powder, he'd very sensibly gone to sleep. Fed, changed, clean and fast asleep in his mother's arms, he looked angelic. I wished that instead of feeling smug that both mother and child were happy, but instead I'd the worry of a looming crisis of Sally on the rampage.

I should have got Maureen out of the kitchen but I hadn't bargained on the bathing taking so long. The sound of the kitchen maid trundling her wagon down the corridor came nearer. She was obviously out of the kitchen and going full steam.

Drawing breath, hand on the doorknob and wondering if she'd left Maureen in one bit, I got my apology ready.

'And it's a grand morning is it not, Matron!' Just outside the door, Sally's voice foghorned cheer and welcome. 'If you're looking for Nurse Macpherson, she's *not* in the kitchen!'

Matron! I'd only a second to register the horror of somebody even less welcome than Sally before the door handle turned in my grip and was flung open.

It was Sally. Her face was so wreathed in smiles, had it not been for the trolley, I mightn't have recognised her. She was beckoning to Matron, coming towards us, as if delighted to see her.

'Look! She's here.' She shepherded Matron into the room, blocking her escape route with the trolley in the doorway. 'I'm savin' you the bother of looking for her, so I am. I know you're a busy woman.'

'And that was very thoughtful of you, Sally. I was just about to start looking for Nurse,' said Matron. 'Thought I might find her in the kitchen.' She gave a mirthless smile. 'But you've put me right, as usual.'

Rather than saying, 'You're the last person I hoped or expected to see. Goodness, don't you ever go off duty?' I opted for glory.

'Ah, Matron. Good morning. I've just been giving Mrs O'Shea here a little help with her baby. Sister MacNutt thought it'd be good practice for mothercraft demonstrations.'

Matron raised an eyebrow and looked at the floor still bearing signs of a recent blizzard. 'Practice is the word,' she said. 'You'd think it'd been snowing. Sally – would you?'

'Right away,' said Sally. 'I'll just nip back and get a cloth out of the kitchen.' I could have sworn that as she turned, she winked.

Matron turned to Mrs O'Shea who was beginning to squirm on her ring. 'So what do you think of Nurse Macpherson's technique then?'

Mrs O'Shea looked down at Connor,

who'd latched onto one of the bed jacket buttons and was sucking contentedly. 'Alright I suppose, but could you tell me, Matron,' she moved like a barge confronting barriers, her brow furrowed in anxiety, 'what's a bairn?'

23

HEADING FOR
THE BRIGHT LIGHTS

'So Sally saved the day?' Although it was morning and we were back in the restaurant, Lorna looked fresh enough to be starting a day shift. 'It must've given you quite a turn though. Lordie, Jane! I don't know how you manage to get such drama going. Next thing you'll be telling me all our single girls are taking their babies home to loving, supportive families.'

'If only that was true.' I remembered sad, tight faces and silent babies. Wraithlike, Maureen had passed on her way back to the ward but at least she'd stopped crying. Compared with Mrs Blair and her judgmental ministrations, Sally must have been kind to her.

Lorna slid off her spectacles and rubbed her eyes, a sign she was tired and mortal after all. 'What did you say to Sally?'

'Nothing. She never gave me the chance. As soon as I went into the kitchen she turned on the sink tap and was up to the elbow in suds.'

I remembered Sally's studied concentration, her red hands swishing bubbles into a huge lather with the steady gush of surely too hot water drowning out any other sound. Her shoulders were set as if fixed and ready for combat. 'I definitely got the message. Conversation was out.'

Lorna yawned. 'And I suppose the same goes for us. God! I'm exhausted. Roll on nights off. I'm dying to get home for some rest and recreation. What will you be up to then, says I to myself, says I?'

'Seonaid's planning a visit to Salthill. Where's that? She's going with Colette, one of her sisters. Asked if I'd like to go too. Good fun apparently.'

Lorna relaxed in her chair and clapped her hands like an enthusiastic audience member. 'Oh! To be sure! That'll be a trip and a half. It's over the border and near Galway. You'll need to tell us all about it when you get back. How're you getting there?'

'Hitching, but don't breathe a word to Marie. She'll spend all weekend on her knees asking for a safe deliverance.'

Lorna chuckled. 'Salthill knows more about parties than most. I hope you get there and, more to the point, get back. It might be difficult if Seonaid's sister's as mad as her.' She looked upward. 'Maybe I'll put a prayer in for you three myself.'

Plainly she had better things to do with her time. As for us, and come late Friday afternoon, Seonaid, Colette and I were standing at a windblown corner of Belfast's road south. It was getting dark and starting to rain. In the chilling drizzle I was marginally cheered by the fact that Sally and I had parted on good terms.

Based on my previous life as a ward maid, we'd bonded in a mutual dislike of people walking on newly washed floors.

Leaning on a mop, Sally had said, 'I can't believe you told Dr O'Reilly to mind where he was going, and even if Sister MacNutt thought you were a bit bold, I've told her I've been dying to do that for years.'

She was full of admiration but I was indignant. 'The least O'Reilly could do was wait till it was dry. You're a key member of the team, Sally, and you work really hard. You keep this place like a palace.'

Seonaid and Colette, however, weren't seeking harmony.

'Would you take that stupid hat off, Seonaid? Nobody's ever going to give us a lift with you wearing that thing.' She glared at the home-knitted hat, without which Seonaid obviously felt incomplete.

Unlike her sister, Colette was tall. Elegant and organised, she tucked a strand of blonde hair back into its orderly chignon, with fingers so white Sally might even have traded her trolley for them. She frowned at her watch. 'I'm going to give it another ten minutes, then I'm off. Would you stop swirling that hat of yours now. You look like a helicopter!' She grabbed the knitted pigtails.

Seonaid hopped easily out of reach. 'Ach, get your leg and thumb out and stop complaining. If you weren't so thrifty, we'd be in a bus and sure, what else would you be doing, stuck in your bed-sit an all?' Apparently Colette's typing job didn't give her the Rolls-Royce accommodation of Bostock House.

Still, she fought her corner. 'I'd not be waiting chilled to the bone and worrying what all this might cost.' She stuck out a lip, thumb and a rather shapely leg. There was an immediate result as a shooting brake creaked to a halt alongside.

Though gratifying, it was slightly marred by both it and the driver's age. Then, too, the amount of slurry smearing the windscreen made it amazing he'd even seen us.

The car hugged the ground. There were straw garnished sacks cramming the boot area whilst a huge bag took up the front passenger's seat.

'Hop in out of the rain! Can you squeeze in the back? This sack's too heavy to move.' There was a leather strap acting as a door hinge. It wasn't very effective but, as he opened the door, the driver seemed impervious to the noise it made scraping on the pavement.

'Now where would youse girls be off to?' In an otherwise toothless mouth a gold-filled one lit up his weather-lined face.

'Monaghan.' Colette, taking in the transport livery, was swift. 'We've family there and they'll be looking for us.' She glanced at her watch. 'Before midnight.'

Judging by Seonaid's surreptitious elbow jabbing, this was news to her as well. 'At least we're heading in the right direction. It's halfway to Galway,' she whispered.

The driver laughed. 'Ah sure, I'll see what I can do and at least I'm going that way.' Then he cranked up and set the wheels in motion, eventually moving from the steady roar of first gear into a second he seemed reluctant to change.

Colette had buried her face in a handkerchief, affected by the car's atmosphere suggesting that McGinty's pig had either left or was about to return. As far as I was concerned it wasn't unpleasant. In the dark it combined with the rhythm of windscreen wipers and labouring car engine in a way that was reminiscent of a ride in the farm tractor at home. Still, conversation was impossible. Eventually, however, a cyclist passed. After a 'What's the hurry?' we moved into third gear and chat.

I said I was looking forward to some sight seeing. I hadn't seen much of Ireland yet but what I had was beautiful.

He was gracious with the compliment. 'Ah, they say Scotland's great too. My wife's been there. Went with the Ulsterbus last summer. She'd a grand time, so she had. I couldn't go because of the farm but I told her to make sure she found out if it was true Scotsmen wore nothing under their kilts.'

Seonaid and Colette leant forward, intrigued. 'And did she?'

The old man chuckled, slapping his hands on the steering wheel, then yanked it to pull away from the verge that was suddenly and frighteningly close. 'Well, she sent me a postcard with a picture of a piper on the front. On the back, all she'd written was F.O.!'

'That was quite a message,' I mused.

'I couldn't wait to get her back home and ask what she meant.'

As if the memory had jolted him into action, the roadside hedges and trees began to pass quicker. Even though it felt as if the car were running on tyre rims, fourth gear began to look achievable.

'She'll not be going back there herself. I'll guarantee that.'

'I'm not surprised,' said Seonaid. 'That postcard must have had you curious.'

His gold tooth brightened the rear-view mirror as he chuckled. 'Well at least hers was satisfied because she now knows about pipers because, what she meant was, she'd *Found Out!*'

As if in glee, he accelerated, but in an engine roar, cloud of black smoke and smell of burning rubber, the car ground to a halt.

Raymond and his car had plainly made Seonaid confident in all manner of mechanical problems. 'That's a flat tyre.' Getting out, she'd pointed to a rear wheel.

Heaving himself out after her, the old farmer inspected it then went to the front. 'No. Look! It's this one.' He kicked a tyre, which by comparison was only marginally flatter.

He was philosophical as, tightening the string round his old raincoat, he readied for action. 'It's a good thing I've a spare and we're near town. See!' He waved in the direction of a collection of lights. 'That's Monaghan. It's an easy enough walk to the centre.'

Despite Colette putting away her powder puff, joining in our combined wish to help and producing a nail file, he was clear that was as surplus as we'd all become. 'Your relations will be looking for you. You can catch up with them at a phone box near Kelly's Bar. It's in the middle of town. And

231

may the saints look after ye.'

With a last twinkle of gold he turned to more important matters.

From a slow traipse into town lightly interspersed with Irish drizzle and sisterly skirmishes we were about to be jerked into a world of music and laughter. It might be getting late but, judging by the light and noise spilling from Kelly's Bar, time was irrelevant. We must be over the border.

Despite Southern Ireland's reputed leisurely approach to time I glanced at my watch. 'I doubt we'll get much further tonight. Galway will have to wait until tomorrow. I wonder if they've rooms here. Let's ask.'

Colette was scandalised. 'Are you mad? Don't even think about it. You must've forgotten me saying we've relatives near here. We'll just stay with them.'

Seonaid looked dubious. 'I know, but we haven't seen them for over five years. And then there's Benny...' Her voice trailed off.

Colette's confidence was awesome – maybe it was her blonde hair or top job in the typing pool. 'All the more reason they'll be pleased to see us. Now, have you change for the phone? I haven't any loose Irish money.'

'Ach! Colette – d'you ever spend money of your own?' Seonaid asked, banging coins into her sister's hand and opening the pub's door. 'We'll be where the action is. Look, there's your man's telephone kiosk,' she said, pointing to a booth nearby. Even in the dark, it was visibly a startling green. 'Use that. Say we're just passing but we'd love to catch up with them and is there any chance of a lift, we've forgotten where they actually stay.'

I figured it might be as hard for them to find us. Kelly's was so smoke-filled and crowded it made visibility eye-stingingly poor. Still, there was no problem locating the music. The place was alive and throbbing with sound.

There was a small stage with a group of young men in leather waistcoats on it. Accompanied by flutes, whistles and fiddles they were giving soul and heart to 'The Rocky Road To Dublin'. Unable to keep up with the words, the audience foot-stamped and hand-clapped with a sound so exuberant, had there been room, we should all have been dancing. As it was, Seonaid did her best. The floor rocked, lamps swung in the swirling smoke and flying barmen crashed full glasses over the bar counter. Guinness contents foamed, brown and creamy, their colours matching the walls.

'Whack follol de rahl!' The group ended the song with a flourish – a pity since a shout of 'Three orange juices' was heard

233

clearly in the lull following the performance.

'A Scot! Can ye sing as well?'

'No. Not unless you want your bar emptied,' I said, carefully reversing from the counter.

'If she won't I will. I know the words of "I Belong to Glasgow",' an old woman cried and, jutting a formidable chin and patting her curls in place, stood up.

'No! Molly–'

Her partner caught at her raincoat, but too late – Molly had escaped. Using finely-honed elbows she cut through the crowd, climbed onto the stage, grabbed the microphone and after a few sepulchral coughs, was off.

She was certainly confident. Then, after delivering a few massacred notes, she meandered towards a higher octave. As if to help her reach it a waggish barman stole behind her and made a cranking gesture.

The crowd erupted but, oblivious, Molly ground on, 'Glasgow' getting further away by the minute and Harry Lauder probably turning in his grave.

Seonaid said, 'You can tell her heart's in it.'

'If not her voice.' Colette had joined us. 'Bet you could do better than that, Jane. She's terrible. Go on! I dare you.'

I saw the conspiratorial look exchanged between the sisters and felt uneasy.

'Not likely and I mean *not* likely.'

At last, Molly ground to a halt and to tumultuous applause was helped off and back to her chair.

One of the barmen looked around. 'Now where's the Scots lass? I'm sure she's something to sing about too. Her friends tell me she's a great wee voice.'

Suddenly made aware that the loneliest place in the world can be somewhere crowded, I cast around for an escape route.

'Come on, Scotty!'

The only place worse was the spot so recently vacated by Molly and which the expectant crowd was now bent on my filling.

24

A HOMER!

Benny might have looked like a shy, middle-aged farmer, but actually he was a hero with impeccable timing. He'd arrived just as I'd crumbled under the pressure of the crowd's good-natured insistence.

'Come on, girl! Just a wee tune now! Sure you can do it. Don't tell us you've come all the way from Scotland not to sing a wee tune?' The stamping of feet and genuine enthusiasm was overwhelming.

I only knew the words of 'The Northern Lights of Old Aberdeen'. Had my city's abortion centre, typhoid-harbouring image crossed the border? Certainly its song, produced in a voice that would have given Molly diva status, made an impending disaster inevitable. Yet the crowd persisted. Slowly I headed towards centre stage.

Then came Benny's voice. Even if it was as soft and gentle as the west wind, it carried, 'I've come to collect three girls, but I'm in a hurry. One of my pigs is farrowing.' He advanced towards the bar counter then drummed enormous fingers on it. 'And I'll take some beer home with me. Seven cans please.'

With the urgency a midwifery team would have accorded a prolapsed cord, the crowd backed off. Maybe the rich aroma coming from Benny's farm boots played a part, but nobody stopped us leaving.

We hurried after the enormous can-clinking figure heading towards a ramshackle pickup van.

'You keep Benny company in the front and we'll just pile in the back,' urged Colette, shoving Seonaid before her. A wind had risen, chasing away the rain and, as the door slammed behind her, causing us to lose what might have been an animated reply. The hat's pigtails went into the blur you get when something's shaken vigorously enough.

'At least she can see out,' I said, cut off from the front by a metal partition and climbing into a space resembling a sardine tin. 'Have we far to go?'

'No. I don't think it's far from here.' Colette was breezy. 'But it'll give Seonaid a chance to catch up with Benny.'

'You seem anxious she should,' I said. 'You're not trying to hook her up with him are you? Even if he's a saviour with great timing, look at that beer he's bought. He might be a bit of a drinker and anyway, he must be your cousin.'

But Colette just laughed and wouldn't say anything until we arrived at the farm and then it was just to make the introductions to Cousin Bridgit whose bright welcome chased away all our tiredness.

'And you'll be staying the night, of course. I've made up beds for you.' She'd the kindly way of a bossy big sister. 'Now you just make yourselves at home.'

She'd hardly finished speaking before Colette and Seonaid were sitting, already slippered, before a peat fire Bridgit had coaxed into action. Confronted by flames flickering gentle shadows on the quiet walls and a sofa's sagging comfort I was tempted to join them.

Instead, intrigued by the old farmhouse with its long mysterious-looking corridor, pitch pine-panelled walls and plain furniture sitting sturdy on stone floors, I followed Bridgit and offered help.

She bustled about the kitchen, clattering dishes with a chef's expertise. Benny was lucky. Bridgit, with her bright eyes and managing way, must be a great asset to any place, not to mention this one. I said so.

'If only Benny'd find a wife,' she sighed, 'then I could find out. But where in the wide world's he going to find one?'

'What would you do?'

'I'd go to England.' Her eyes shone as if she were talking about the end of a rainbow. 'I'd join the rest of the family. They've all done well over there.'

'We've crofter bachelors at home,' I said, 'and they seem to manage fine, and if they don't, they buy help.' Bridgit looked thoughtful, as if it was a radical concept. I reckoned Benny would think so too, but he'd sped off into the night saying Verity needed his help.

'Ah, sure but she's not doin' too well.' Bridgit sighed and flapped her hands by her sides in frustration, 'That pig's an overfat, lazy, ungrateful oulde sow. I'm thinkin' she's forgotten she's havin' anything but a good night's sleep.'

'Could I go and see? I'm from a farm myself.'

'And here training in midwifery.' Colette's voice came floating through. 'Two midwives!

How's that for timing? And hey, Seonaid! You should go too. You might pick up some tips.'

Verity's sty had a cosy feel conspicuously lacking in the Royal's labour ward. I don't suppose labouring women would have appreciated a straw bed, but there was a simple, uncomplicated feel to the place they might have preferred. An overhead-heating lamp gave it such a rosy glow it made you want to nestle up with the patient. She, however, merely gave us a measured look and grunted.

Plainly Benny felt we were surplus to requirement. He addressed his remarks to Verity, but she ignored him in much same way as he disregarded us. 'Come on now, Ver. You told me you were ready. And now you're just lying there. It's time you were moving.' He stroked her ear as if to encourage her listening skills. Verity shifted restlessly. If she'd been a woman she'd have slapped his hand.

'I think she's getting bothered.' Bridgit had arrived with a bottle of Fairy Liquid. She thrust it at her brother. 'Here! You'll need this.'

Benny looked doubtfully at us then consulted Verity. 'I'm hoping you don't mind an audience. The ladies might be thinking I'm a bit bold, but I'll need to find out what's happening inside.'

Throwing herself into the spirit of the dialogue, Seonaid bent down. 'Don't you be worrying about us. You'd never imagine what us girls have seen already.' She sounded competitive.

Benny went as pink as Verity. 'Oh well, here we go. Steady, girl!' Soaped from his hand to the armpit and all but disappearing, he reached up the pig's rear.

A couple of barn cats, drawn by the activity, arrived, took a ringside seat, pulling their tails about their feet as if cold, but giving Verity and her warming lamp a respectful space.

Colette would be far more comfortable. Since farrowing knowledge wasn't a clerical requisite it meant she could stay inside toasting her feet by a fire and putting night cream on a flawless complexion instead.

She was spared a dead pig.

'Cord round the neck!' Seonaid was shocked. 'Ah God!' She was on her knees and spoke with such pity, for a moment I thought she might perform the last rites.

'Don't!' Maybe so did Benny.

But Seonaid was scrambling back. This was very sensible given that Verity's maternal instincts might at last be galvanised into action as, following the corpse, lots of healthy little squealers emerged. As if desperate to escape the first one's fate, leave their confines and gain the attention of a previously moribund mother, they came quickly.

'Twelve! Now isn't that grand. A celebration it is then.' Benny, positively loquacious, was wreathed in smiles as, holding onto one beer, he poured the rest into a handy pail.

Seonaid and I exchanged glances, worried we were going to be offered a swig. But Bennie was catering for Verity. 'You'll be thirsty after all that hard work and,' he surveyed the piglets plugging into their mother with gusto, 'you'll be needing it and...' he popped open the remaining can and went to sit amongst the new family, 'if I may, I'll join you. Keep you company for a bit. Come on, cats.' He patted his lap.

'He's just checking Verity doesn't get hungry in the night and start eating her pigs. He'll be there for the rest of the night,' explained Bridgit as she showed us to our bedroom. 'But you should sleep well and there'll be a good Irish breakfast ready for you in the morning. How many sausages?'

When she went away, Colette returned to her favourite theme. 'Ach, Seonaid, would Benny not be a catch? This is a fine big farm, lovely house. You'd never be hungry and he's only a cousin twice removed. You'd be helping Brigit too.'

'No.'

'Why not?'

Eyes gleaming, Seonaid sat up in bed, exasperated, then hissed, 'Benny's too old and so's this house. It's full of ghosts. Can't you hear them?' Impossibly, her spiky hair was standing even more on end. Her face was shocked and white. 'Listen!' She cupped an ear.

Then she lay back and disappeared into a deep sleep, leaving a host of creaks and groans to creep about, conspiring to ruin ours.

At least we heard no more about Benny and didn't see him the next morning either. Seonaid reckoned he was hiding but I wondered if he was still tucked up with Verity. He'd soon wake up once he knew his sister was composing a *'housekeeper wanted'* advertisement she planned on putting in the local paper.

It was late when we got to Salthill but we found a Bed and Breakfast easily enough with a landlady who worried neither about ghosts nor security.

'The door's never locked, you can come and go as you like,' she said, ushering us into a bedroom where pink bedspreads screamed abuse at a wallpaper so busy with spots it was bound to give anybody, never mind a phantom, a migraine. It was hard not to switch the dazzling electric light off before our hostess left the room.

There'd been times when I'd wondered if we'd ever get here. A combination of old lorries, battered cars and circuitous routes by kind strangers wanting to show us beauty spots had taken us far from the main route. It might have been quicker hitching a lift from the horse-drawn gypsy caravans. Loitering along the roads with a tangle of children and dogs scattering happily about the wheels gave a feeling of elegant, relaxed progress.

We could, of course, had we time, have taken a ride on the donkeys that roamed the roads like free spirits, apparently ownerless and unchecked. Their presence lent a gentle charm to rural scenes where stone dykes stitched grey seams into a countryside, velvet-soft in every shade of green.

Still, what was a scenic tour compared to the bright lights of Salthill and which our landlady was now keenly promoting. 'We're in a grand position for O'Connor's. You should go there. You'll enjoy it for sure. Just go out the door and follow the sound of music. It's great craic.'

She was right. The pub had the same vibrant charm as Kelly's but with the additional look of a local museum. Every conceivable space was crammed with a jumbled eclectic mix of pictures, old lamps, barometers and farming utensils. There was just enough room left to dance with music provided by an accordionist group so joyful it made our feet itch.

'Don't leap too high or you might brain yourself.' Colette pointed to the lamps hanging from the rafters but Seonaid was off, partnered by a thin intense-looking bloke in a shiny blue suit.

Maybe he couldn't keep up with the pace of her flying heels. Instead and shortly after taking the floor, he seemed keener to draw her away to engage her in vehement chat in a quiet corner. He'd a nervous way and kept pushing back a lock of hair as if to make a point. He looked really interesting and Seonaid was listening hard until he searched in his pocket to draw out a small metal object.

Suddenly, with an abrupt shake of her head, she stood up, gesturing to us to join her in leaving.

'Jasus, Seonaid! What's all that about?' Colette demanded as we stood in a surprised huddle outside the pub. 'I've left my drink in there and it wasn't cheap.'

'Ach never mind about that. Me heart's goin' like a hammer and I'm tremblin'. Feel that,' Seonaid, stretched out her wrist. 'Take me pulse, Jane!'

'Mmm, you're alive.'

Disappointed, she snatched back her arm. 'It's racing, and not surprising either. Your man back there's just shown me a bullet. A bullet!'

'Mother of God!' Even Colette was impressed. 'Where would he get that?'

'He says he's plenty. When he heard we worked in Belfast, he asked if I could give him contacts. Says it's time for a United Ireland. He showed me that bullet to prove he was serious.'

The music from O'Connor's swirled and eddied about us. It was a happy, exuberant sound yet it couldn't chase away a fog of unease chillingly settling about us. Salthill had seemed such a cheerful place. Seonaid's encounter with a man who spoke of unity and bullets said something else.

I offered, 'Maybe he was joking and he did seem to be on his own. Look, I don't know about you, but I'm whacked. Why don't we just go back to the Bed and Breakfast? It's been a long day. Things will look different in the morning.'

And for once there was no argument.

Compared to last night's menacing undertones, an early morning's sisterly wrangle sounded positive and healthy. Leaving a godless person to sleep on undisturbed, the girls had gone to catch early Mass. Their return was less discreet.

'Ah, Colette, I can't believe you took two shillings out of the collection plate.' Seonaid sounded outraged.

Colette had the injured voice of the righteous. 'What else could I do? I only *had* two and six. I could only afford sixpence.

Anyway, I might need money for getting home.' She prised open her purse, eyed its contents then snapped it shut. 'Somebody round here needs to be careful.'

There were no further sightings of the purse until we were returning home. We'd had a lift from a lorry driver who was going as far as the official border: a casual affair.

As we got out, Seonaid pointed to a man selling something. There was such a roaring trade for it, a queue of people had formed, waiting their turn. 'Look, they've got oysters. What about having one?'

'No!' Colette said unsurprisingly.

'I've never tasted one,' I said. 'What are they like?'

'They're two shillings each, and a delicacy. Very tasty Oh, let's each buy one. Just to finish off the holiday. Go on, Colette, you'll be wanting one when you see us having ours.' Seonaid was in full cajoling mode. Maybe she just wanted to see the purse being opened.

'Oh well then. Might as well, but it better be good.' With some ceremony, Colette took out her money and grudgingly handed it over. Pleased, Seonaid trotted off to come back shortly after, a smile on her face, three shells in her hand.

'Is that them?' Colette was shocked. 'You really mean we only get one each?'

'How do you eat them?' I was curious.

'Swallow in a oner,' said Seonaid.

'I'm going to chew mine.' Colette was adamant. 'I'll never get the taste of such a little thing otherwise.'

Seonaid had tipped hers into her mouth, smacked her lips then wiped them on the back of her hand. 'Mm!' She eyed her sister as she dithered with hers. 'Would you hurry up!'

Colette opened her delicate mouth and held the oyster, savouring the moment whilst Seonaid looked on.

There was a pause, then – 'Yuck!' She suddenly threw it away in horror.

Pointing to it quivering on its shell, her sister had mused, 'Does it not just look like a dirty big snotter?'

25

LOOKING TO THE FUTURE

Miss Harvey was like an exasperated general dealing with a Home Guard group incapable of marching in time. In her classroom, the last place it intended practising, the class fidgeted and squirmed.

Marie was clicking her rosary beads and in

a world of her own. So was Seonaid – probably thinking up new ways to annoy Colette or Matron, having recently been sent to her for another lecture, this time on time keeping.

'Ah, sure it doesn't worry me so much now,' she'd shrugged. 'I just opened my eyes wide, trained them on Matron's left ear, looked surprised then checked my watch. I thanked her for being so keen to advise me, and I mustn't be late for getting on duty. She got rid of me far quicker than the last time I was there. I bet it was to check herself in the mirror.'

'I think she's a beautiful person. I often visit her,' Margaret had said by way of comfort. 'Just for a chat, you know.'

'I'd say an evening with a boa constrictor would be more fun.' Lorna breathed on her spectacles to clean them then put them on, magnifying her twinkle.

Marie whispered, 'Sure, and I don't think that'd be a nice pet to keep. Mammy would have a fit if I took one home.'

Maybe that was what was now occupying her thoughts.

As the class continued with its own thoughts and aware concentration was elsewhere, Miss Harvey lost her cool. 'Would you please pay attention!' She knuckle-rapped the desk. 'In two weeks, you'll have your theory and clinical exam. You'll also need to have all of your record books completed.' Her voice dropped to the tones of one discussing a dear departed. 'Of course you know everything's going to depend on you passing these exams for you to move on to Second Part. Our consultant obstetricians will be taking the clinical part.'

Aware she now had complete attention and eye contact no longer a problem, she moved into full military mode, hardening her jaw and speaking slowly and very clearly. 'They'll be expecting a professional presentation so it's up to you to find out all you can about your patients. As you should know by now, confinements here are based on a likelihood of complications so you need to be on the lookout for anything and everything. Understood?'

'Yes, Miss Harvey.'

She seemed sufficiently pleased with the response to hand out prizes. 'Practice is the key word so I've arranged for you to go as a group to the antenatal clinics. That should prove invaluable.'

'We've been there!' chorused Margaret and Cynthia.

'Well a little more experience won't do you any harm, as I'm sure you'll agree, Nurse Smythe.'

Cynthia, minus double barrel, was plainly out of favour but it didn't stop her squinting down that splendid nose. 'Can't I go to the labour ward instead? I'm short of normal deliveries. I'll need them to get my record book completed.'

Margaret couldn't resist it. 'Goodness, haven't you got them already? I've had mine for ages but if you like I could come and help you.' Her laugh was easy and designed to annoy.

'I sometimes wonder if I'm dealing with adolescents or grown women,' said Miss Harvey with a heavy sigh.

There was the same problem in the ante-natal clinic as our class checked in at the same time as our arrivals. A pretty young girl came first, closely followed by a similar version, if faded, a bit crumpled, and carry-ing fully loaded shopping bags.

'Have you come to help your daughter?' I asked, searching around for a seat and somewhere to put her stuff.

'No. She's here for her first but I'm a regu-lar. I've come for a checkup on my twelfth.' Patting her coat, she sounded preoccupied and more interested in checking the bags.

Taking in our conversation, Annie, the clinic midwife, said, 'Maybe you could look after Mrs Quinn. Take her details. She doesn't need to be hanging about. She'll need to get back to her kids. Let her get the weight off her feet on that chair there.' She pointed to one at a row of desks where

Seonaid had already settled and was beckoning to Mrs Quinn's daughter.

We took the one beside her. Seonaid was patting the case note files stacked before her as if she couldn't wait to get started. Taking up most of the desk space was a line up of blood pressure machines, test tubes and enough syringes to stock a factory. Unfazed, our patients waited their turn, chatting amongst themselves as if at a village pump, whilst those heading for the desks seemed completely relaxed.

Mrs Quinn, however, wasn't up for giving either chat or her medical history.

'Every time I come here, I get asked the same question,' she complained as we ploughed through a questionnaire dealing with everything but intended holiday plans. 'And no, sure I don't remember the date of my last period. I don't think there's been one since she was born and she was my first.' She nodded at her daughter.

I looked across. Seonaid and her patient seemed to be having an animated conversation. How come, I wondered, they had so much to speak about with only one intended pregnancy when here we were in multiple numbers struggling to fill the boxes.

'Twins in the family?' I asked.

Mrs Quinn consulted her shopping as if it were an abacus.

'Two sets.'

There was a burst of laughter beside us. I felt I was letting Mrs Quinn down in terms of jokey asides but two sets of twins was a sobering prospect. It couldn't have been easy getting here, and how on earth did my patient look so tidy?

I was full of admiration for her stoic calm. I blew a strand of hair to clear my vision and squinted down at her feet. Observation was one of the key skills Miss Hardie had harped on about and ankles were a good barometer.

Those neat ones with their feet shod in polished leather promised fair weather, not to mention an ability to walk on water, whilst at a higher level her face was miraculously full of purpose and life.

Dr O'Reilly appeared but not even his good looks and charm made her blood pressure anything but normal.

'Ah! Another of my regulars,' he said, placing a hand on her shoulder. 'I'll be having a look at that bump of yours once the nurse here's weighed you.'

Maybe she was used to always being lumbered one way or another or the shopping bags carried something important but, even without clothes and about to be weighed, Mrs Quinn took them with her onto the scales.

Relieving her of them I said, 'I think your daughter's ready to go now. Could she take those with her?'

'Surely, but tell her to get them to Sadie right away. She's my neighbour. It's her shopping but so run over with children she's no time to do it.'

'She must be glad she's got an organised friend and, as for your daughter, an experienced Mum must be a boon.' I was full of admiration.

'Ah now, she learnt it all at her mother's knee a long time ago.' The tone was practical whilst she adjusted the headscarf she'd refused to remove. 'But I'll be telling her,' she pulled the scarf ends into a very tight knot, 'to be sure and train her husband better than I ever did mine.' She swung onto the examination couch with lithe ease.

'Quite right,' said Dr O'Reilly, 'and maybe I could have a word with him too. But in the meantime, d'you mind being a guinea pig for Nurse Macpherson? Her tutor tells me she's needing a bit of practice before her clinical exam, so I need to lead by example.' He made a great show of rubbing his hands. Then, once they were suitably warmed, he smiled and said, 'Perfect temperature. I wouldn't want cold ones making you leap off the couch. I'll go first shall I?'

'Help yourself.' Mrs Quinn settled back as if she was being offered four-star accommodation whilst Dr O'Reilly investigated her bump with his thermally correct hands. 'Interesting,' he pronounced, eventually stepping back. 'What d'you think, Nurse?'

There was quite a lot to look at. Then, putting a hand on her abdomen, even more to feel. It took me ages but I got the impression that Mrs Quinn was housing a tenement full of busy residents.

'Well?'

Our patient, perhaps absolved from the responsibilities of parcel minding or probably from the length of time I was taking, had dozed off.

'Double trouble?' I whispered, wanting neither to upset nor wake her.

'Right!' He nodded approvingly. 'But there's only one sure way to find out. I don't want to worry her. I mean there's two sets of twins already so just tell her we're trying to find out how far on her pregnancy is. You'll need to take her down to the X-ray department. Once done, be sure and come back with the films quickly. We don't want to hold back a busy mother. Don't mention twins until we know for sure. Wake her up, but gently now. If we tell her about twins she might have a canary.'

'As well as or instead of?' I asked, delicately shaking our patient awake. The X-ray department was nearby in a small unit on its own but apparently connected by telephone to the General Hospital. Two receivers sat on the reception desk beside a small handwritten notice that said, 'In the absence of a radiographer phone two-three-two-zero.'

Refreshed by her little snooze Mrs Quinn wandered over to some randomly-placed chairs and started to marshal them into rows. As I lifted the phone and dialled I wondered if she was counting them.

'Do you do X-rays for the Maternity?' I asked when someone answered the phone.

'I'm not sure. Just hold the line.'

There was a short pause then the second phone rang. I picked it up and, the other one being occupied, put it to my left ear.

'Maternity X-ray department,' I said, to which came back a familiar voice. 'We've just had a caller asking if we do X-rays for Maternity. But we don't, do we?'

'I'm not sure,' I said, aware I was repeating her response to my original question.

I was now as confused by having a telephone at each ear as I was conversing to the same person on two phones. Any moment now she was going to come back to me on the other line. Maybe I should disguise my answering voice. That would fool her!

'Phone two-three-two-zero and they'll keep you right,' were the instructions.

I must have dialled the wrong number.

I'd have liked to apologise but she'd put down her phone. I should have done that too. I'd have avoided the radiographer. She was back, plainly from a fag break and was curious to know why both telephones were being commandeered, and by a mere nurse.

Mrs Quinn thought so too, 'Maybe you shouldn't leave silly scraps of paper with squiggly figures on it. They're not one bit clear. The poor wee nurse has been all but phoning herself. She must've thought she was talking to a fool.' She lined up pencils on the desk and, squaring a notepad beside them, stepped back to admire her handi-work. 'Now! That's better.'

The radiographer seemed mollified and chuckled. 'The numbers are there to get a radiographer over here. I was only out for a minute but already you've got the place tidied up. It hasn't been so orderly since your last visit, Mrs Quinn. Now let's see if you're as tidy inside.'

Dr O'Reilly took the X-ray films and held them up to the light.

'Uh-huh.'

'What news then, Doctor?' Mrs Quinn asked, trying to get a look.

He looked apologetic and held up two fingers.

'Ach, Doctor, is it not me that's had the practice?' she said, brow clearing and show-ing a rare glimmer of humour. 'You had me worried for a while. Did you not know I'd be having twins? I could have told you that already.'

26

MARCHING ORDERS

Margaret looked as if she was heading The Glums' Club. Even Marie, our usual Captain Doom and sitting beside her, looked marginally cheerier.

Close enough to be within earshot, I muttered to Seonaid, 'That pair look as if it's the end of the world. Who'd want to bring gloom sitting in this nice sunny dining room. Look, I'm starving. Let's sit somewhere where they won't put us off our food. Having exams so close as well, I'd like to be some place more cheerful.'

But I was too late. Already Seonaid was skipping towards their table.

'So what's the craic? Youse look as if you're going to a funeral.'

Margaret was usually a stickler for etiquette. Now she was slumped across the table, crumbling a piece of bread over her plate and idly mopping it up with a huge chunk of butter.

'Ach, Seonaid, you were right about that oulde Matron after all. She's a heartless woman. Not a bit of compassion in her whole body.' Carelessly and with the back of her hand, Margaret wiped her buttery chin.

What more proof could there be that something was wrong?

'And sure Margaret only meant to help.' Marie was as defensive as if we were already arguing. 'And it was only about safety, wasn't it?'

'It was Brian, actually.' At least using his name perked Margaret up a little. She straightened up, righting her shoulders. 'I was sure I should tell Matron he thought that having an oxygen cylinder tied to the back of a bike might be dangerous. And being a policeman, he should know.' Her sniff was profound. 'I thought she might be grateful for a safety tip.'

I thought Margaret should either have her head examined or get a medal for bravery whilst Seonaid wondered aloud if it was any old bike or was Brian talking specifics.

'District ones of course,' snapped Margaret. 'That's what the guard at the back's for. The basket in the front's for our black bags, and Brian thinks even they could make experienced cyclists wobble about.' Her large capable hands gave an exaggerated wiggle.

'If we need oxygen I'd think we were in trouble,' I said. 'I didn't think Belfast was that hilly. I'd hope to manage without any help, and won't we need baskets to put the babies in? I mean we are supposed to be delivering them aren't we?'

'Ah, Jane! You're teasing us.' Marie was reproachful. 'The oxygen's not for us – it's in case the babbies need it, and you must see how upset Margaret is. You're not helping with your wee jokes.'

'Never mind.' Seonaid pointed as Cynthia in full sail swept towards us. 'Here comes Happy Legs. She's bound to cheer us up.'

'Dear God! She's all I need,' moaned Margaret.

'I've something to pass on,' declared Cynthia, sitting down, expanding her chest and readying for an announcement, but Margaret, eyes blinking, excused herself and hurried away.

Cynthia looked after her in exasperation. 'Honestly! She's going to miss my news and it's important. Anyway, what's wrong with her?'

Marie gulped. 'Matron's after telling her it's probably best she leaves after sitting First Part. She says she's always worrying about something and now Matron's had enough of her moans and troubles. She's a busy woman with a hospital to run, without nurses, never mind policemen, coming to tell her how to run it.'

Coming from Marie, this, without a mention of God, made an impressively strong statement.

'That woman's determined to get rid of us all,' sighed Seonaid. 'You'd have thought Margaret would be her star pupil. Responsible and all.'

Cynthia was finding it hard to be gracious. 'So much for always popping in to have a chat. Speaking personally, I've always found one's best to keep one's superiors at arm's length.'

Torn between thinking Brian might have a point and wondering how we could filch an oxygen cylinder to do a practice bike run with one on board, I went for the usual put down. 'Does one indeed!'

'Yes, and anyway Margaret can do Second Part somewhere else. There's lots of choices. I've actually got a friend joining us to do hers here. I'm looking forward to it. She's quite a card and...' Cynthia twitched her nose as if this was a strange concept, 'rather good fun. Actually we're thinking of moving into a flat. Get away from that awful woman MacCready, and before I forget, that's what I've to tell you.'

Looking round as if she wanted a bigger audience, she drummed her fingers on the table in exasperation. 'Margaret's just missed this bit of news. A pity. She'll not expect to find men fumigating her room.'

'Men!' Marie's scream had perfect pitch.

'Why?' Seonaid asked, beginning to show more interest.

'I just mentioned to her I'd delivered a woman covered in lice. I'd wondered why she was wearing a cap, but she was delivering so quickly I didn't have time to put one on myself. I just asked MacCready if she had any insect repellent in case,' Cynthia shuddered, 'any had landed on me.'

'And had they?' Already I felt my skin crawling.

'Of course not! But of course *she* carried on as if I'd brought infestation to the entire Home and to our floor in particular. As I speak, she's on red alert with everything, but men are coming to fumigate our rooms and, get this, they could well be wearing breathing apparatuses.'

Seonaid screwed up her nose. 'It's well that I never told her about my last delivery then. My wee mother I was delivering was moving, now, *moving* and when we washed her hair all that happened was the nits hatched in the warm water.'

Marie seemed lost in devout contemplation, doubtless sending up a prayer for God's poor, the unwashed, the lost and the lice.

Behind the service counter Daisy was promoting tattie scones. They were a favourite of mine but not enough now to keep me at the table. Cynthia was sitting that bit close whilst Seonaid, with slapping hands, was imitating someone covered in fleas.

Appetite ruined and trying not to scratch, I rose. 'Thanks for that, girls, but you'll have to excuse me. I think I need a bath.'

27

A PROFESSOR CALLS

'And how're we feeling today?' asked Lorna as if a class full of ashen faces and nervous chat was an everyday norm. 'And Margaret, you're surely not thinking of visiting church?' She pointed to her watch. 'You'll hardly have time. Our practical exam's any minute now.'

Margaret, loitering at the classroom door, was wearing a suit that had all the brown style and charm of a monk's habit. Neither lipstick nor eye-shadow adorned her pale heroic face. Even the wings of the big butterfly brooch pinned to her lapel drooped as if sad, knowing that flight was impossible.

'I'm not doing it,' she said. 'I'm only here to wish you all good luck and say goodbye.'

'What rubbish!' Miss Harvey, brisk and business-like, suddenly appeared at her shoulder. 'Go and get changed right now and hurry up. You haven't much time and we don't want the consultants waiting, do we?'

But Margaret's compass was set on martyr-dom. 'Matron's said it's best I leave.' Her lips quivered. 'So that's what I'm going to do. I don't want to waste anybody's time.'

Miss Harvey's native Scottish thrift was plainly outraged as she rolled her eyes and spoke slowly and very clearly. 'Well you'll certainly be doing that if you leave now. And after all my work and effort putting you through First Part? Now that is a waste! Don't be such a silly girl. Go and get changed. Quickly now! Or your examiner won't give you the same chance.'

'Oh, well if you put it like that,' Margaret said, throwing in the towel. Scarlet-faced, she slunk off, whilst our tutor, dealing with the day's first challenge as easily as flea bites, gave the rest of us the names of our patients and where we would find them.

'Nurse Macpherson. You'll find Mrs Scullion in Sister MacNutt's ward.'

'But that's Post-Natal!'

'I think, Nurse, you'll find your patient's expecting you as well as a baby.' Miss Harvey was in no mood for argument so, notebook in hand, heart in my mouth, I hurried to the ward assuming Pussy would relocate me. Instead, and appearing as if from nowhere, the soft-footed Sister pointed to the side ward I'd last seen occupied by Mrs O'Hagan.

'*Missus* Scullion,' she said, stressing the title as if it was my patient's most important feature, 'is ready for you. Now why would that baby be crying?' She disappeared into the nursery where, very quickly silence reigned. Pussy's soothing voice often had that magical effect.

I could have done with the same treatment. I'd also have appreciated it if she'd said Annie Scullion was not only married but was a mistress of mirth too. A chorus of laughter flooded into the corridor as Sally, opening the door, trolley-reversed out.

'Great to share a joke, and that one's a cracker, so it is, Missus. Now,' she leant on her trolley, 'you be sure and tell this wee nurse that one. She loves a laugh. Oh! But you're a caution...' Tucking a stray grey lock under her cap's anchorage, she kept the door open and said in an encouraging way, 'You'll both be grand, so you will.'

Had it been anyone other than Sally I'd have said she left with a skip in her step. She must have swapped the bleach bottle to concentrate on lavender polish. She'd certainly been busy with it. Its smell triumphed in a room freed from clinical restraint. Flowers brightened every corner whilst the room's occupant flashed the same wide smile as the two youngsters in the silver-framed photograph on the locker beside her.

The open window gave out onto a tree in full May blossom. Sunshine, joining in colour, poured gold in to what was apparently the room's resident sunbeam.

Her tanned face may have made her eyes especially blue, her teeth a gleaming white, but only good health could be responsible for that clear skin and shining blonde hair. She looked like a Swiss dairymaid advertisement. What on earth was she doing in hospital?

There was certainly nothing wrong with her athleticism either. Mrs Scullion jumped into bed with gazelle-like grace. She sat up, clutching her knees as if to stop them bouncing her out of bed. 'Holy Moly! Is this not a grand honour! Never did I think I'd be grand enough for a student's final exam but now, here you are. Wait till I tell Michael. He'll be sure to die laughing.'

'Michael?'

'Me husband. He's staying at home looking after the children. Says he never thought it'd be such hard work.' She gurgled with laughter, then added, 'So you'll be looking to see what's wrong with me?' She snuggled down as if waiting to hear a good story. 'See if it's any different from Mr Coles.'

I wrote down the name carefully, glad to have something to put down on paper.

'And he's your consultant. Like him?'

'He's great. Lovely man. Wears a three-piece suit and all. Says I've to stay here for a wee rest.' She slapped her hand over her mouth. 'Uh! I'm not supposed to say that, am I?' Merriment shivered the blankets. 'Wait till I tell Michael.'

Aware of the Professor's imminent arrival, I examined my patient from head to toe. Maintaining a degree of sobriety under fire from her giggles interspersed with remarks on my resemblance to Dr Finlay's Janet and what she would tell the long-suffering Michael, I hurried on with questions about her previous and present pregnancy, all singularly lacking in problems.

Other than a dose of the giggles, a very early bleed and an expected delivery in three weeks, Mrs Scullion appeared to be in robust health and worryingly up-beat about being in hospital.

'Such questions!' she said, clapping her hands and flashing her dimples. 'I'd never have thought the half of them. Anyway, I wasn't going to challenge Mr Coles about coming here. Well, he's a consultant, isn't her?' Anyway, I'm having a grand holiday and Michael's finding out about child care.' Another gust of laughter and a flash of very strong teeth. 'Mind, you've been very thorough. You'll be bound to pass.'

I remembered Miss Harvey's lecture stressing that there must be something unusual for somebody to be admitted here. I grew anxious. I went over my notes, picking out a few anomalies much the same as clutching at straws and was about to say, 'OK. I give up,'

266

when the Professor arrived.

With a sinking heart I made the introductions.

Sobered either by his air of gravitas or watch chain, Mrs Scullion assumed an air of quiet suffering. She looked out the window, apparently more fascinated by the pink-blossom view than the findings of her pregnancy I so laboured over and was now presenting to the Professor.

He was unimpressed.

'But what else?' He sounded tetchy. 'It sounds like a perfectly normal pregnancy to me.'

I knew it was hardly riveting stuff. Mrs Scullion had so lost interest she stretched luxuriously and yawned largely. I went over the details again, slowly. At this rate and with a bit of luck, I might just bore him to death.

Instead, he grew irritable. 'I know, I know. Heard it all already. What else have you found?'

I'd only one trick left in my bag. Mrs Scullion swore it was her first clue to pregnancy.

I hadn't thought I'd need to use it but it was certainly a surprise aspect to my patient's history. Miss Harvey had never mentioned the condition and I didn't think it appeared in any midwifery textbook. Maybe then my patient was here to make medical history. Ah ha!

I took a deep breath then, trying unsuccessfully to modify the Scots accent and like a conjuror producing a rabbit, announced, 'She's got a wart in her ear.'

At least I'd surprised the Professor. Robbed of speech, he'd gone puce.

Still, Mrs Scullion had convinced me and I *had* seen the wart. I said, 'That's how she knows she's pregnant. It goes once she's had her babies.'

'And I suppose you'll have diagnosed this one's sex dangling a ring over her abdomen.' At least the Professor's power of speech, if not colour, had returned.

'Indeed, and who'd be listening to that oulde wives' yarn?' A small cloud scudded over the bright countenance of Mrs Scullion, now completely awake. As if he posed a threat, she folded her hands protectively over her bump. 'And what would you know about it anyway? You're not even my doctor!'

This was bold talk and plainly not what the Professor was used to. In a flustered way he thanked Mrs Scullion then, exiting the ward with a lot less grace than Sally and her trolley, he suggested he and I find somewhere more private.

In a small room, and now safely away from a peasant's revolt, the Professor resumed his inquisition.

'I'll have to ask you again, Nurse.' His voice rose and his eyes narrowed in an alarming way. He really was cross. 'Was there anything else you found out about your patient?'

I groaned inwardly. There was nothing for it. I'd tried everything and still hadn't come up with the right answer.

Seriously in want of a vital clue I sent a silent message to my career-sorting angel. Get on my case! Otherwise Margaret's not going to be the only one about to leave.

'I couldn't find anything really wrong with Mrs Scullion.'

'Precisely!' The Professor gave a shout of triumph. He could hardly contain himself or the waistcoat buttons heaving under the strain of his emotion. The watch chain quivered. 'At last! It's so obvious. Wouldn't you agree, that woman's a bed blocker, Nurse, nothing else?' Had he been a lesser mortal, I'd have said he spat the words. Certainly I hadn't been expecting that reaction.

Even if I wasn't sure what he meant I was anxious not to put anything in writing, so I just nodded.

'Her consultant's keeping that bed for one of his private patients. It's a dirty practice and I'd like it stopped. This is a National Health Hospital and should be treated as such.'

Soundlessly, magically, Pussy appeared. 'Are you nearly finished?'

'We certainly are,' said the Professor, obviously just as pleased to see her. 'We'd have been done ages ago had I not been fobbed off with some fool tale about warts.'

'As a sign of pregnancy, d'you mean?' Pussy chuckled. Her soft accent, so efficient with the babies, was blessedly having much the same effect on my examiner. His waistcoat buttons settled back and his face resumed a normal colour.

Pussy said, 'Come on, Prof., let's have a nice cup of tea and we can both have a good moan about consultants and how the National Health Service is abused nowadays.'

As they went, her voice floated back, 'You wouldn't have been giving Nurse Macpherson a hard time would you?'

The Professor's reply was lost as the office door banged shut.

I was really relieved. For a giddy moment I'd thought Pussy was about to enfold him in those long arms and tuck him up in the Nursery.

28

ON THE ROAD!

It was the end of the first six months. We'd completed the course, sat all its exams then, to our relieved astonishment, all passed. Second Part beckoned.

I was looking forward to it. The memory of the nightmare interview with the Professor was already receding but, even with a hundred per cent success rate, we'd failed to impress Miss Harvey.

Calling up her native instincts, well-honed in doom, she'd said, 'Don't think you can rest on your laurels. You must realise you're only qualified to take more responsibility. You'll be out on District with little or no medical backup and you should certainly know by now that childbirth can be anything but straightforward. Remember the lecture the Professor gave you right at the end of First Part?'

He'd been very keen on hospital confinements, listing with discernible relish a catalogue of problems that could attend home ones. 'And you might be the only one around to deal with them,' he'd said. Then, as if fearing we still hadn't got the message, he'd added, 'If you were dealing with a burst appendix, would you take it out on a kitchen table?'

When Cynthia and Margaret chorused they might if they had to, he was appalled. 'That's the thing, though. The point of your skill is to ensure your patient gets to hospital if she needs to. Now *you* might choose to keep her at home,' he pointed an accusing finger at Cynthia, who puffed her cheeks as if she might go into orbit, 'but I, as a fully-qualified surgeon, would ensure she got the best of treatment in the right place. Hospital!'

Hopefully not to practise surgery by stealth, Margaret had gone to be a staff nurse in an Antrim hospital. I wondered if Cynthia missed her. We did but were happy she'd gone for a bright and sparkling future with Brian, who'd been transferred there.

'Antrim's got a nice wee racecourse, so it has,' Seonaid had said. 'We'll come and meet up with you and Brian. Have a cup of tea and go on to have a wee flutter. Sixpence both ways maybe.'

Knowing my pal's notion of hospitality might involve someone else in full scale catering for an unlimited period of time, I thought a day at the races was the least of Margaret's problems. But she was happy, waving a finger and watching her engagement ring catch the light.

'Sure. Why not? At least I won't be the one getting into the saddle.'

Thinking of the Royal Maternity ones, I thought it was a pity we'd all failed to get Margaret cycling proficiently. She was going to miss the joys of tootling about Belfast on a bike, free from hospital's constraints, with the privilege of seeing patients and getting an insight into their lives at home.

I was as excited on our first day on District as I was when first called 'Nurse'. Desperate to saddle up and get going, I couldn't believe it when told that our first lecture concerned our bikes and their maintenance.

Sister Marks was in charge of the District unit. She was young, dark and pretty, with a nice line in dry humour. She delivered the talk in the bike shed, flashing an old battered jotter before us. 'This is the Accident Report Book. You'll need to read it and hopefully learn from other people's mistakes.' She pointed to a bike chain with a finger carrying a suspicion of grease. 'I expect you all know the basics. Pumping tyres, checking brakes and so forth, but if this comes off, I'm presuming you'd know how to put it back on?'

I nodded vigorously. This was easy! I'd been riding a bike since I was a kid. Loving the freedom two wheels could provide, I fancied I'd be the class's cycling expert.

'Good,' said Sister Marks, noting my confidence, 'but mind, biking can be dangerous, especially on busy roads.' Her tone was light but I was disappointed.

The vision of effortlessly sailing along the Falls Road might need refining. Even if it did recognise a caring person on a bike, there was no guarantee traffic would scream to a halt to allow her to go about important duties.

We leafed through the book, astounded by its litany of disasters. One in particular grabbed our attention. 'Furniture removal reversed into bicycle, thereby causing some scratching to the paintwork.' There was no mention of the rider.

'Nice that they look after the bikes so well,' said Seonaid with caustic humour.

'I'm thinking Margaret had the right idea after all.' Marie's face was puckered in worry. 'I never thought cycling would be so hazardous and I was really looking forward to a wee spin.'

'Nonsense!' I got hearty. 'You're the one who was dying to get on a bike. You'll be fine. Remember, the trick is to go at a steady pace and look ahead. Keep your eyes on the road. Now, come on! Sister Marks has given us directions to get to that GP's antenatal clinic. Apparently it's at a surgery. If we don't get moving, we'll miss seeing the patients.'

We steered the bikes out of the shed. From a previous encounter, I should have remembered they were so heavy they needed the care of handlers dealing with skittish colts. Maybe the front baskets carrying our black bags, laden with everything from a foetal stethoscope to a puncture repair kit, affected the steering but those steeds were intent on going everywhere but on the road.

'I'll either have to grow or get a lower seat,' Seonaid said, looking at her bike, its saddle at her eye level. 'I can't reach mine. Would there be an adjustable spanner anywhere?'

'Here! Let me,' said Sister Marks. She took a thing like a monkey wrench from her pocket and, with a deft flick, reduced the seat's height in a second.

Seonaid swung on, held the brakes then stood on the pedals. From an unaccustomed height she was looking down on us. 'Right! Let's go.'

'Tally-ho, ting-a-ling and forward!' agreed Moira, Cynthia's friend. She was a welcome addition to our class and popular with her ready laugh and sporty outlook. She even made Cynthia lighten up. I could easily cope with the fact that she'd been blessed with a lean figure and curly red hair, but I really couldn't manage her fronting the group now heading for the Falls Road.

This was surely my field of excellence. With the urgency of a despatch rider, I pedalled hard after her, determined to be leader.

We'd been given uniforms of lugged caps and navy blue gabardine coats. Mine kept flapping open and acting as a drag because, in my haste, I hadn't tied the belt. Still, I managed to get past most of the others and overtake Lorna, pedalling with the professionalism of a careful driver, and close to the front. She pulled down her ear flaps and pointing to them shouted, 'Handy if you break the sound barrier, but what's the hurry?'

Ignoring that as much as my thundering heart's protest under pressure, I pushed the pedals harder. The sky was blue, the sun was warm and flashing past the others had given me a surge of triumph. The distance between Moira and myself was shrinking fast.

'Nurse, Nurse, I'm getting worse but mind where you're going,' a small boy called from the Falls Road pavement. In an exaggerated way he threw himself against a shop window as if he was in danger of being run over. I was too breathless to reply but now drawing parallel to my quarry.

It was so easy! I must be going very fast. Either that or she was slowing down. With a casual wave I sailed past her.

She'd looked shocked. Leadership, I figured, surely couldn't be that important to her, then with some surprise I saw a bus stopped in the middle of the road. Cars were beginning to stack up behind it.

I rang my bell and began to overtake them. The drivers might well think I was heading an emergency team. Maybe with a little practice our class could learn to cycle in formation. As leader, I'd show them it was easy.

I looked back to see if the girls were following but instead they were so far behind I could only see their open mouths and gesticulations. They seemed to be shouting but I couldn't hear them. This was a pity.

Had I been concentrating on looking ahead, I'd have seen the coffin bearers making for the Falls Road cemetery. Following them and taking up the entire street was a group of mourners on whom I was now bearing – with no exit strategy in mind.

29

A BIT OF A NIGHTMARE

I'd arrived at the surgery, energy so spent I had to use the bike like a zimmer frame. I was still trying to get my breath back when Moira arrived.

Looking like a healthy-living advert, she slung her bike against a wall. 'I can't believe you didn't run anybody over!' She sounded almost respectful. 'When you did that crazy zig-zag round the coffin bearers, I thought you were going to either fall off or take off.'

She took deep and apparently energising breaths whilst looking round as if savouring the view of raw liver-red buildings crammed closely together. 'I do so love a bit of exercise. Such fun!'

Any minute now, I thought, she's going to start running on the spot. With her bright cheeks and sparkling eyes she looked ready for another six miles. When it came to stamina, Moira was the outright winner.

Just managing to straighten up, I wheeled my bike alongside hers. Between wheezes I explained, 'As soon as the coffin bearers heard me shout it was an emergency, they gave me enough space to get by. No wonder I got here first. I'd to keep up that breakneck speed until well out of their sight.'

'You're telling me. I'm only here on account of your slipstream,' chuckled Moira. 'I've never followed anybody jet-propelled before.'

Remembering the coffin-bearing group wheeling round in well-drilled formation out of harm's way made me feel guilty because I'd lied about an emergency, but I was honest when I said, 'Belfast folk are wonderful. Even the mourners flew to the side so I could get past.'

The others arrived, Seonaid taking the lead in mockery. 'Some emergency! Even if you were really far ahead, we still heard you.' Her imitation was frighteningly accurate. '"Keep your eyes on the road!" Eh?'

As the girls, sniggering, parked their bikes they kept a watchful eye on a cluster of children nearby. Whilst four were making a game of jumping off the surgery steps, one surely just out of nappies was jiggling a well-used pram to try and soothe its bawling occupant.

'Shouldn't at least some of those children be at school?' said Cynthia, frowning at the tallest who was orchestrating the step lift-offs.

Shouting 'Higher now, higher!' she was, despite the pudding bowl haircut, very pretty and very young.

Cynthia, apparently immune to the charms of a group with all the vitality and aimless grace of leaves blowing in the wind, said, 'With them around I wonder if it'll be safe leaving our bikes here.'

'I shouldn't worry. Any minute now, they're all going to be air borne,' said Lorna undoing her earflaps as if to hear better. 'Sure wouldn't their laughter break your heart?'

By now, the minute baby minder had moved from rocking to hanging on the pram handle. It obviously presented ideal leverage, if not balance, but made the infant, a less adventurous spirit, scream louder. Any minute now that pram was going to topple over.

We moved in but weren't as quick as the grey-haired woman coming out of a nearby butcher's shop and sprinting to the rescue.

With bike or not, it's amazing the ground you can cover if needed, I reflected. Even though she was carrying a large parcel and was wearing slippers and a stride-defying tweed skirt, the lady could shift.

'Ah, Granny! We never thought you were coming. Can we go home now?' asked the eldest, having a last leap and joining the breathless woman who was hanging onto the pram much like its last minder.

Apparently deaf to the sound of an infant bawling, the woman seemed more concerned with getting her breath back but at last she managed to utter, 'Ah, Deirdre, your Mammy won't be long.' Then, as the children gathered about her, she showed them the parcel. 'Look, a nice neck of mutton, so it is. We'll all go home and start to make the tea. Something nice for your daddy.'

'Must be the da's ma,' whispered a cynical Lorna.

All but Deirdre piled into the pram, their waving arms and legs making it look like an octopus on wheels. As the woman pushed it down the road, Deirdre, her short blue frock blowing about her skinny legs, kept one hand on the handle, 'One day I'm going to fly,' she said, hopping to miss the cracks on the pavement, 'if I practise enough.'

They disappeared. The street, despite having people on it, seemed drained of vitality. Then Sister Marks screeched up in a Mini, providing noise if not colour with her car the blue of a sulky sky. Had it not been for the red of her uniform peeking out from under her grey coat, she'd have been lost in the drab surroundings. Wherever we were, I thought, this sure wasn't Belfast's leafy suburbs.

Quickly checking a kiss curl in the wing mirror, Sister Marks apologised for being late. 'At least I see you lot managed to beat the traffic and get through that funeral hold up. Let's go in. Come on! They'll be waiting for us.' She raced up the steps two at a time, then bounded into the surgery.

We followed with Cynthia bringing up the rear with a little more dignity. 'It's easy to see she didn't have to cycle here,' she grumbled, then stopped, astonished. 'Good gracious!'

She'd just seen what had startled the rest of us. Inside and waiting in a group of antenatal patients was Deirdre; only older. With the same angular body, high cheekbones, dimpled chin and thin legs the resemblance was extraordinary. The difference was that Eileen Ferguson must have had a bigger bowl for the haircut, was Deirdre's mother, and was shortly to have her sixth baby.

So soon, in fact, that a couple of weeks later I was in a taxi heading for her house. It was the middle of the night and my first time on call. I'd never thought I'd sleep but Sister Marks had had to shake me awake.

'Get up!' she hissed with a lack of finesse impressive in someone of the caring profession. 'Mr Ferguson's just phoned. I heard coins clinking so he must've been in a kiosk. You'll need to remember that, and give him time to get back to it so he can tell me when she's nearer delivery. At the moment, she's just started to feel uncomfortable so just you go and assess her to begin with. They don't live that far from here so I'll soon nip out. I know it's your first delivery but you'll be fine and you know her from the antenatal clinics, which should help.'

'No problem,' I lied, throwing myself out of bed thinking it was just as well our overnight accommodation was in the single-storey District unit. Had I been in Bostock, I might have jumped from the seventh floor instead.

Still I wasn't having the nightmare Marie had on her first delivery.

Whereas my taxi driver actually knew where Eileen's house was, on Marie's delivery she'd been called by a community-based midwife she didn't know, to a patient she'd never seen. She had no idea where she was going – neither did her taxi driver, and it was two in the morning.

For some time, he'd said nothing. He just drove for what seemed to Marie to be ages and in increasingly frustrated circles. Eventually he'd snapped.

'Wee bastards!' His cry banshee-screamed through his open window but the huge and faceless housing estate through which they were driving responded not one iota.

Marie had come back to the unit ashen-faced and, though she had been up all night, very wide awake. 'Ah, girls!' she reported. 'I thought he meant he hated babies so much he might just throw me out of his taxi for delivering them.' Her wide-eyed gaze encompassed the class. For once we were all attentive and, anxious to avoid a similar experience, hanging on every word.

'And what did he mean?' asked Moira, scratching her nose, a sign, if rare, that she was anxious.

'He wasn't one bit friendly but all he meant was there were little tearaways who pull down street signs. So he didn't have a clue where we were.' Marie sighed as if in absolution for someone who'd nearly given her a heart attack. 'We did get there eventually, but if it hadn't been for one house light and the midwife sending neighbours out to look for us, I might still be in that taxi.'

'Well! If we're called out in the middle of the night I can't think why we don't just use our bikes,' said Moira, stretching her arms as if readying for a warm up. 'From what you're saying I think we'd get there just as quickly.'

Seonaid, her imagination activated by reading a lurid murder thriller, all but screamed, 'In the middle of a dark, dark night? You'd never know who was lurking about. I can't believe you've just said that. Ach, sure, but your head's cut!'

Moira must have looked blank because Cynthia explained, 'It's the Belfast way of saying you're off your head and actually I think, Moira, she may have a point.'

Coming back to my own call out, glad enough not to be relying on two wheels, I still wasn't all that happy about it. Yet, there was something pleasant about being carried safely through Belfast's silent streets in a taxi. Enfolded in a cocoon of warmth and gazing straight ahead, I wondered if the driver needed to clear his windscreen. Visibility didn't look that good.

I hoped this wasn't a precursor to fog. Unlike in Aberdeen where a horn moaned its sick-cow message to the universe, the Belfast one didn't seem to have the same range. Occasionally, silently, chillingly and unexpectedly, a cold mist would sneak into town. It would linger, killing vision, muffling sound and staying like an unwelcome guest until a temperature or wind change came to lift its depressing presence.

There was more than a suspicion of it as I glimpsed a window, its light slightly haloed, in the street where we now stopped.

'This is us,' said the taxi driver, nodding at a man hovering outside, 'and there's the Da. Poor thing, he'll be worried sick.' He wound down his window and sniffed the air. 'I'm thinking I should get home now. I don't want to get caught in fog. It comes so quick too. Ah but it's the very divil!'

Before I could get a chance to see my patient and convince her that, in the interests of safety, she should be whisked into fog-free hospital care, the taxi with a crash of gears was gone, its shape swallowed into the night, its tail lights blurring into the distance.

Silence dropped into a damp and menacing air.

There was nothing for it. I was in charge.

'Quick deliveries a speciality.' I held up my black bag to the ridiculously young-looking man whose face broke into a smile.

'Ah, the wee Scots girl! My wife said she hoped it was you. She said you're great craic, so you are.'

He couldn't have said a more worrying thing.

30

GOING SOLO

Unlike Marie, I'd seen my patient a couple of times at the surgery. She was only a year older but I couldn't imagine myself coping with five kids, never mind looking forward to another. I respected her in many ways, not least because she was happy to acknowledge her mother-in-law and the help she gave.

'My own mammy died in childbirth,' she'd explained on one of her visits to the clinic. 'I don't know how I'd manage without Dermott's. But she's getting on a bit now. We thought it'd be easier for everybody if I'd this babby at home.' She'd grinned. 'The children've hardly got used to the last one and it's an awful work getting them ready for a hospital visit. At least if I'm at home, they'll see this wee one when and if they want *and* it'll stop them thinking babbies only come from hospitals.'

'I suppose you've sometimes thought that yourself,' I'd answered, 'and it's no use saying it's the light that's attracting them but...' I'd dared to say, 'after this one's born, what would you think about taking the Pill?'

She could have been offended. Instead she'd looked thoughtful. 'It's really against our religion. It's difficult, but we're supposed to use the rhythm method.'

I'd raised an eyebrow and did a boogie movement whilst spreading my fingers over her bump as if it was a piano. 'Safer moving on the floor.'

'As well?'

'No, instead.'

She'd laughed but said she'd have a word with Dermott. But right now might not be the best time to ask if she had. Probably not. Dermott was more welcoming than any hospitable host as he ushered me into the cramped hallway of an unnaturally quiet house.

I wondered how such an obviously small home managed to accommodate so many people even though most of them were little. 'Have you gagged and bound the wee ones?'

Dermott, scrubbing a mass of black hair too luxuriant for any bowl to cover, considered the question seriously. 'No. They're with my ma,' he said, opening a door into a living room, 'but they've left their linen.' He pointed to small garments drying in front of a blazing fire and a clothes-horse on which nappies hung as if it were a flag day. 'I'm trying to get them dried before tomorrow.'

On the mantlepiece standing beside an ornate, if stopped, clock was a jar of Thovaline, a cream to stop nappy rash. Its pot was blue and matched the colour with which someone of artistic bent had painted two of the tiles on an otherwise drearily brown fireplace. Even though the linoleum was the same drab colour, the wallpaper with its peony rose sprays made colourful splashes on a navy background. The house may not have been grand but it was warm and felt welcoming.

'Now, Nurse,' Dermott said, rubbing his big knuckled hands together. They made a sound as rough as sandpaper on wood. Like a squaddie about to take orders, he straightened his shoulders. 'Eileen's upstairs. I've looked out the delivery pack and put the kettle on.'

'Good. Two sugars please and no milk – I'm trying to diet.'

Eileen seemed remarkably cheerful for someone in labour. Wearing a thin nightdress, she sat by the window on a hard chair, resting her feet up on another.

'What's it doing out there? Dermott said it was a bit misty.' She pointed to the faded blue-velvet curtains, efficiently blocking out the night.

'The stork might have a problem locating Belfast,' I said, hoping I was wrong. I handed

288

her a thick mug of tea much the same colour as the lino. 'Dermott's finest.'

Ignoring the weather report, she said, 'He makes a grand cup, so he does,' and drained its contents in one.

It wouldn't have been like this in hospital! Once patients were in the labour ward they wouldn't be fed. Fluids would be limited to the odd ice cube, essential liquids given by an intravenous drip. It made the patients safer candidates for an anaesthetic if needed: and thirsty.

Eileen wouldn't be that. Plainly fortified, she now pointed to a bulky package on top of a wardrobe masquerading as an upright coffin. 'It looks like a Christmas parcel. Dermott put it there out of the children's way. We've had a terrible job keeping them out of it.'

'I think they'd have been disappointed,' I said and took it down, unpacking it quickly. Disregarding spotlessly white dressing towels, a pack of sterile delivery hardware and enough cotton wool to cocoon an elephant, I searched out a plastic sheet. 'Look! This'll keep your bed safe.'

'I'll give you a hand,' she said and winced as she stood up.

'Just you stay there.' I'd noticed a small telephone under the bed. Phew! I must've dreamt Sister Marks said there wasn't one in the house.

I pulled it out and put it in a handy place. Between Eileen looking increasingly uncomfortable and a growing anxiety that the taxi driver might be right about fog, I might have to make that call soon.

I patted the bed. 'Come on, Eileen, let's have a look at you.'

At the first sight and palpation, I instantly knew something was wrong. What should have been the head pointing downward was too small. Higher up, something as large as a cricket ball bobbed. How, I worried, had I not picked this up at the clinic?

'Have you been having pain under here?' I touched the bottom of her rib cage.

'How'd ye guess?' Eileen was plainly impressed. 'Is that a crystal ball you've got in that black bag of yours?'

I reached for the phone, already dialling. 'No, but maybe it's time to get Sister Marks here. Hello?'

I was surprised, then torn between worry that Dermott answered and relief that Eileen wasn't having a convulsion. She was only laughing. 'You're a card, so you are!' She wiped streaming eyes. 'That's the children's phone. Their other one's downstairs.'

Pretending I wasn't fooled, I was casual. 'Convenient though.' Then wondered how I could convey the urgency of my message without alarming either parent. 'Um, Dermott, could you contact the district unit and say to Sister Marks the baby shouldn't be long but might be coming bum first.'

There. I'd said it. I checked my watch. Silence. I waited for an anxious scream from downstairs and in the absence of one, felt tempted to provide it, but Dermott just said, 'Right you are, Nurse. I'll be as quick as I can.'

It was as if I'd ordered another cup of tea.

A wedding photograph of Eileen and Dermott sat on a dressing table. From a tarnished silver frame they smiled a little doubtfully over the pile of nappies and baby clothes surrounding them. If they'd known their future, I thought, checking my watch and hoping Dermott would be quick, they'd have looked a lot more uncertain.

'If it's bum first, will that be easier?' Eileen began to move restlessly.

I was cautious. 'Everything will be fine as long as that baby of yours reads the signs on the way out, but if there's any problems we'll easily pop you into hospital.'

Eileen looked worried. 'Ah sure and I don't want that. Ow!'

I hoped I was presenting a calm front whilst desperately reviewing a mass of knowledge about breech births. In hospital, I recalled, some were straightforward enough but if a leg came first there was no guarantee the other would accompany it. A problem for an obstetrician then! Turning the baby to come headfirst might have been an option – if I'd been that same obstetrician and sure the baby wouldn't strangle itself on the umbilical cord.

At least, I comforted myself, the bag of waters hasn't broken. The baby was safe inside it and this was hopefully a sign that its bottom was sitting over the exit like a snug cork. If it were the first part to arrive, the rest would be more likely to follow in an orderly way.

There was a picture of a placid-looking Madonna nursing a rather chubby Jesus on the wall. I had to keep calm but, right now, she was holding the serenity card.

Sick with apprehension, I put the foetal stethoscope in place.

The baby's heartbeat was as reassuringly steady as Eileen's faith. 'It'll be grand, so it will. Mary'll look out for us. Mother of God!'

Her womb muscles, lax from previous labours, were now beginning to protest. From the record of her previous births Eileen's labours were getting quicker. Then, frighteningly and rapidly picking up steam, her progress from first-stage labour to second was so extraordinarily fast there wasn't time even to discuss a painkiller.

A door banged. Then, from the bottom of the stairs, Dermott shouted, 'It's a pea souper alright, but Sister Marks got the message. Says help's on the way.' His voice was drowned by a yell that would have wakened the dead. 'But,' he finally added as he came upstairs, 'I'm thinking by the sound of it, it won't be needed.'

'Great!' I said. I only meant the baby's bottom had emerged, but given the circumstances I was delighted to see that part of a baby's anatomy.

Would I tell the parents they'd a boy?

Waiting, heart in mouth, I recalled watching a similar breech birth and its subsequent slow progress in labour ward. It was particularly memorable since Sister Flynn, that mistress of time management, had astonishingly decreed, 'A breech this far mustn't be rushed. We may have to sit on our hands if we feel like interfering.'

Then the mother had been brought to the end of the table. I was worried that even though only a part of the baby was hanging over the edge, it looked a risky position. Sister Flynn had just scoffed. 'Well, as you can plainly see, the midwife's there to hold it. We're just tapping into the law of gravity so that it's a gentle descent. You'll see that baby will come out in its own good time. All we need to do meantime is to keep an eye on the foetal heart and the cord free of tension.'

Tension! The term might be out of context but, here in this home confinement, it could just as well apply to me as well as Dermott, who'd just arrived.

'Jasus!' Ashen-faced, he stared round-eyed at his son's bottom. 'Is that a cyst I'm seeing, and what's Eileen doing so near the end of the bed?'

He put his hand on the back of one of the chairs I'd given Eileen so that she'd something to put her feet on and make a better position for delivery. For a moment I thought Dermott was going to sit down but, obviously made of sterner stuff, he was only steadying himself.

'What's he talking about? Honest to God, Dermott, there'll be no more children after this,' said Eileen between groans. 'It was never like this in hospital. Stop gawping and get up here and support me back. It's killing me.'

'But everything's going well, you're halfway there,' I said, trying not to croak. 'But Dermott, you'll need to give me a hand. Are yours clean? Can you make a long arm and pass me that cloth?'

Opening his eyes for a moment and now peeping over Eileen's shoulder, he grabbed a towel and threw it over.

I held it so that the emerging body would have a clean supportive landing – then waited. And waited.

Dermott gave a loud sigh, then, pale but going for heroics, he opened one eye and said, 'Could we not just pull the wee fella out?'

'No! You'll put his head into the wrong position. We've got to give him time.' I tried to keep my voice from trembling. 'Honestly, Dermott. Trust me.'

'Sure she knows what she's doing,' offered Eileen between groans, 'but it's dreadful sore.'

'I'll never put you through this again,' swore Dermott, plainly searching for action – and that is what he got shortly after when all hell broke loose.

With dawn making a tentative appearance and his mother's yell competing against the sound of a blaring siren, more of the baby came into view. A few more anxious minutes and then the back of his head appeared.

'Now, we can do something,' I said. 'One last wee push, Eileen!'

Holding his body over my arm, I put a finger in Master Ferguson's mouth and, with my other hand keeping the back of his head flexed to allow him easier passage, gently lifted him out. 'And look! We've got a safe arrival!' I felt faint with relief.

'Is he alright?' Eileen was anxious. Doors were slamming, there was shouting and footsteps pounded up the stairs. The only silent person was the baby.

'He's going to be fine.' In the absence of oxygen, I blew air on his face and cleared his nose and mouth. 'Just can't get a word in. Pass me that dish with the scissors, will you,

Dermott, I'm going to cut the cord.'

As if distressed at the sound of scissors so close, the baby gave a tiny but mutinous cry.

'Ah! The wee dote,' sighed Eileen as Sister Marks ran into the room.

'That's a great sound,' she said, relief written all over her face. 'Did you hear us arriving too? Sorry we're so late. That fog's murder. Here! Let me.'

'We're managing fine. We're a great wee team.' Dermott, cloth in hand, took the baby. 'And what a grand pair of lungs he's got.' Cradling him with expert ease he moved to the top of the bed. 'Look Eileen, our wee son!'

'I feel redundant,' mused Sister Marks, 'and here's me bringing the Flying Squad with all their emergency equipment. Maybe I'll just go back with them and leave you to finish off here. Would you be happy enough with that?'

There couldn't be a better opportunity! Charged by success and relieved that the third stage was underway, I said, 'Of course, but before you go, Sister, we were discussing this being the last baby – for a while anyway. I've been suggesting the Pill to Mrs Ferguson.'

Dermott looked horrified. 'The Pill?'

You'd have thought I'd suggested ready abortions.

Sister Marks drew breath and moved into the sweetly reasonable mode of one professional to another, if less believing. 'It's used by a lot of women nowadays. Doctors only prescribe it for women who have irregular periods. Of course, regulating them is important if you want to practise the rhythm method.'

'Well that would be alright then,' said Eileen. 'Are there many who are on the Pill then?'

'Yes,' said Sister Marks with a wry smile. 'You've no idea how many Irish women are being identically treated for the same problem.'

31

WHAT NEXT?

'You were lucky you'd no more breech births during your district training,' said Matron, looking up from the sheaf of papers stacked on her desk.

Lucky! I wondered if I should point out a few strands of white hair only noticed after Master Ferguson's birth. At the end of the course, unlike the ageless Matron, I'd probably got a few more, but compared with promoting a wart as a reliable pregnancy test and delivering a breech birth, the final exam of our Second Part had seemed easy.

Now, one more hurdle remained: an interview with Matron to discuss our future.

The day had started with us nervously waiting in the classroom. Cynthia had been first in line. Lorna, a late arrival, reported seeing her coming out of Matron's office after a very short interview.

She said, 'I think Cynthia may have fallen at the last fence.'

I got cold feet. Cynthia of all people!

Lorna continued, 'Poor girl! Her meeting with Matron doesn't seem to have gone very well. Either that or she's getting the flu. She's all red-eyed, with her face stuck in a hanky.'

Moira, furiously scratching her nose, said, 'I bet she's told Matron she wants to be a ship's nurse. Not what Matron would want to hear, I bet. That woman can be cutting enough to reduce a cat to tears and Cynthia won't have liked getting a row.' She paused and looked thoughtful. 'You know Matron's looking for some new staff midwives? Well I imagine the idea of someone gadding about the high seas wouldn't come naturally to her, least of all when it's our Cynthia jaunting off.'

'I wouldn't have thought it either,' I said, relieved that Cynthia's future actually sounded quite hopeful. 'I bet you'd something to do with that.' But Moira was already bounding off for her interview.

Seonaid came skipping in. She was highly triumphant after her session with Matron. This was not only comforting but something of a miracle.

I said, 'You seem to have got on alright. How on earth did you manage that?'

Seonaid's high kick constituted a health hazard as she chortled, 'Ah sure, she must be desperate to get staff. She said I'd matured so much since the beginning of my training, she offered me the chance of being a staff midwife here.'

'And what did you say to this wee miracle?' Lorna wondered.

'I said "no thank you". I'd be waiting for her job once it became vacant.'

'Mother of God! You never!' Marie went pink. 'What a nerve you've got. By the time she gets to me she's going to be raging. Raging now! Ah, girls! What d'you think she'll say when I tell her I'm going to Uganda?'

My advice was quick. 'Easy! Just say you're fixed up. Going to a hospital. What's it called again?'

'Villa Maria. It's near Masaka and run by nuns.'

'Simple. Just tell her you're going home. You don't have to say it's in Africa.'

Where had Marie's sense of adventure come from? Looking at her resolute little face, I felt dwarfed by her unsuspected courage. I'd never have gone to the missionary fields. All the same, going home to add District Nurse training to my Midwifery part seemed tame by comparison.

The Professor would not have approved, but I'd found life on District hugely satisfying and richly rewarding. I'd learnt that Belfast by bicycle gave a better view than the sometimes grim one glimpsed through a bus window. Visiting the homes of a warm, generous, hard-working, fun-loving, family-minded people made me feel part of their lives. Caring for people at home was so much more rewarding than hospital! But I could hardly say that.

Searching for a suitable alternative I was grateful that at least Lorna was before me. She was keen to stay on and Matron would be daft not to let her.

Plainly, and judging by Lorna's upturned thumb as she came out of the office, Matron thought so too.

And now it was my turn and I still hadn't come up with a cunning plan.

'So, Nurse Macpherson,' Matron leant forward. 'Breech births? You wouldn't want too many like that.'

Not waiting for an answer, she patted the papers, then steepling her fingers, leant back in her chair. 'I imagine you'll be going back to Scotland?'

Even if I didn't want it, where was the offer of work? Matron had completely taken the wind out of my sails. Moira and Lorna having fitted the bill, she must have torn up further job offers.

'You're not going to be like your friend Nurse Fitzsimons and tell me you're waiting for my post then?' She gave a faint smile, then in a patronising way and using a shockingly bad Scottish accent. 'So, you'll be off to your wee But and Ben instead?'

'Er, no.'

I looked around the small immaculate office where the windows giving out onto the hospital grounds offered a better view than the walls, all bare but for one shelved with books.

'What then?'

My eyes fell on a blue one lettered in gold, prominently displayed – Matron's book.

I sighed. Resting an elbow on the desk, I took a deep breath then, what was certainly the plunge, said in the matey way of one on equal terms, 'No, Matron, I'm thinking of writing a book.'

The publishers hope that this book has given you enjoyable reading. Large Print Books are especially designed to be as easy to see and hold as possible. If you wish a complete list of our books please ask at your local library or write directly to:

Magna Large Print Books
Magna House, Long Preston,
Skipton, North Yorkshire.
BD23 4ND

This Large Print Book, for people
who cannot read normal print,
is published under the auspices of

THE ULVERSCROFT FOUNDATION